The Saga of Hávarður of Ísafjörður

With an essay on the political, economic and cultural background of the saga

E. Paul Durrenburger and
Dorothy Durrenburger

Published by Hisarlik Press, 4 Catisfield Road, Enfield Lock, Middlesex EN3 6BD, UK. Georgina Clark-Mazo and Dr Jeffrey Alan Mazo, publishers.

Copyright 1996 Paul and Dorothy Durrenburger

All rights reserved. No part of this publication may be reproduced, stored in a retrieval system, or transmitted, in any form or by any means, electronic, mechanical, photocopying, recording or otherwise, with the prior permission of the publisher and the copyright holder.

British Library Cataloging-in-Publication data available.

ISBN 1 874312 19 2

Printed in Great Britain by Watkiss Studios, Beds.

CONTENTS

Acknowledgements ii

The Political, Economic and Cultural
Background of *Hávarður's Saga*
    Introduction 1
    The Story 4
    Political Economy, Literature and
        the Social Order of Medieval Iceland 7
    The Structure of *Hávarður's Saga* 15
    The Ideology and Practice of Honour 25
    Sagas and History 32
    Translation Issues 36

The Saga of Hávarður of Ísafjörður 43

References Cited 98

ACKNOWLEDGEMENTS

Hjörleifur Jónsson, Nicola Tannenbaum and Jeffrey Mazo read previous versions of this work and provided valuable suggestions. Readers should not blame any of them for any part of the work they do not like.

The Icelandic language has some letters that English no longer uses, especially Þ,þ ("thorn") and Ð,ð ("eth"). The first is like the th of the English *thing* or *thought*. The second is like *th* of the English of *this* or *that*. We retain the Icelandic letters to preserve the sense of Icelandicness of the text.

The Political, Economic, and Cultural Background of *Hávarður's Saga*

INTRODUCTION

In the ninth century chieftains from Norway began to settle in Iceland with their slaves, followers, and livestock. The people of Norway of that time were just beginning to experiment with forms of governance we call states, and those who went to Iceland avoided such developments for another four hundred years. Neither society resembled modern nation-states. The differences are significant and important because we tend to view all societies through the cultural lens of what we consider normal, and all who read this book are members of nation-states, societies in which nation-states provide the backdrop and assumptions for everyday life. While radically different from modern societies, Iceland's society was not unique—Europe had been filled with such social orders for millennia (see e.g. Odner 1974) and we have anthropologists' accounts of similar societies from Africa, Asia, the Pacific islands, and the Americas.

A copious anthropological literature testifies to the complexity, genius, and richness of systems of law, tradition, and discourse among people of all societies. The level of cultural sophistication and complexity does not vary with degree of involvement with modern technology or global political-economic power. While the term has long been debated for its negative connotations, anthropologists have often referred to societies without state organizations as "primitive." Medieval Iceland was one among many primitive societies.

Medieval Iceland exhibited its own unique characteristics, as all social orders, segments of societies, and individuals do, just as it shared common features with other primitive societies. From the twelfth century, Icelanders began to write the documents whose remnants now define a intricate and variegated literary-historical tradition. If we understand these documents as the remains of a society's account of itself, they can tell us much about medieval Iceland and other such societies.

While anthropologists typically learn about primitive societies by ethnographic fieldwork, we learn about medieval Iceland from its literature, much of which was written in the thirteenth century. Interpretation of the stories of the literary-historical tradition suggests that Iceland was first permanently settled in 870 AD, a date generally confirmed by archaeology. Chieftains founded a general assembly in 930 AD, and at the assembly they accepted Christianity in 1000 AD as a result of an arbitrated settlement between disputing pagan and Christian factions. There were feuds and strife from the time of settlement, but they became more severe in the twelfth century and culminated in a period of brutal warfare now known after the most powerful family throughout most of the period, the descendants of Sturla, or the Sturlunga, as the Sturlung age. This ended in 1262 AD, when Gissur Þorvaldsson began to represent the king of Norway in Iceland as his earl and the chieftains began to cede their chieftaincies and become subjects of the king.

For the most part medieval Icelanders wrote about their own society. They collected a group of materials about ancient and contemporary customs in a work called *Grágás*. They recorded the chaos of internecine warfare in the thirteenth century in a series of writings later collected and called *Sturlunga Saga* and wrote sagas about their Christian bishops. One prolific writer was Snorri Sturlason, a chieftain who composed a manual for the interpretation and composition of poetry and a history of the kings of Norway. He was eventually assassinated by Gissur Þorvaldsson. Other medieval texts include sagas of Norwegian kings, a grammar of the Icelandic language, and a compilation of ancient verses. From the twelfth century we have a short history of the first two hundred fifty years of the settlement, and a collection of accounts of the first years of the settlement of Iceland called

Landnámabók (The Book of Settlements). There are also church writings and annals. Among these surviving texts are the family sagas, most of which were written in the thirteenth century about people and events of the time from the settlement of Iceland in the ninth century to the twelfth century. While we know the authorship of some of the medieval literature, the sagas are anonymous, and it seems unlikely that, in the absence of evidence, any amount of debate can establish who wrote them.

From 870 until 1262 AD Iceland was a stratified society without a state. It is this fact that makes medieval Iceland interesting to anthropologists, as some maintain that such societies are very unstable. In stratified societies, one group of people claims privileged access to resources at the expense of others. Fried (1967) argues that such societies either create the institutional apparatus to guarantee privilege—states—or the disadvantaged would assert their rights against the others and institute the equality of access to resources that characterizes most societies without states—primitive societies.

In Iceland, a stratified society without a state persisted in a marginal environment for about four hundred years, calling into question Fried's idea that such orders are inherently unstable. Such societies characterized Europe for a long time even while states were being established. The medieval literature of Iceland, especially the family sagas with their stories of disputes, feuds, marriages, negotiations, settlements, raids, and rich genealogical contexts, offer anthropologists native accounts of the Icelandic social order and the ways in which they interpreted their past.

Anthropologists have discussed such traditions for more than a hundred years. Morgan described medieval Icelandic kinship in 1871 and others have continued to be fascinated with the topic (Rich 1989). Bertha Phillpotts used saga evidence for an analysis of kin groups in a 1913 work. Marcell Mauss quoted *Hávamál*, an ancient wisdom poem, as a text on reciprocity in the opening of his famous essay on the gift in 1923. Lewellyn and Hoebel drew parallels between Cheyenne practices and medieval Iceland in their classic 1941 work on law. Rosalie Wax and Laura Thompson wrote on medieval Iceland in the late 1960s, and Victor Turner and

Knut Odner followed in the early 1970s (Durrenberger 1989). More recent work by anthropologists includes E. Paul Durrenberger's *Dynamics of Medieval Iceland* (1992) and volumes edited by Ross Samson (1991) and Gísli Pálsson (1992).

In addition to this anthropological work, there is a massive literary scholarship devoted to the study of various dimensions of the writings of medieval Iceland (Clover 1984; Clover and Lindow 1985; Byock 1982, 1984, 1988; Andersson and Miller 1989; Miller 1990; Pálsson 1992). Bruce Gelsinger published an economic history of the period in 1981. In the past few years social history has become more prominent in saga scholarship and some have taken up the theme of the construction of social meaning in language use as evidenced by the medieval literature (Jochens 1993).

There are about forty-five family sagas of various lengths, of which perhaps the most famous is *Njál's Saga*. Some sagas such as *Eyrbyggja Saga* and *Laxdæla Saga* center on particular geographical areas while others, such as *Gunnlaugur's Saga*, *Kormákur's Saga* and *Egil's Saga*, feature warrior-poets, while still others, such as *Gísli's Saga* and *Grettir's Saga*, are about outlaws. *Hávarður's Saga* is one of the family sagas. We present the saga here because it is has not been easily accessible in English and because it illustrates many interesting sociological, political, economic, and cultural dimensions of medieval Iceland—both the earlier period, the setting of the saga, and the later period, when it was written.

THE STORY

The main characters are introduced in formulaic terms common in the sagas: Þjorbjörn Þjóðrekursson is an aristocrat of dubious character; Ljótur, his brother, is as bad; Hávarður is an old man who has been a great viking in the past but now, past his prime, lives with his wife, Bjargey, and his maturing son, Ólafur; Þormóður is an unpopular shape-changer.

After the round-up of sheep in the autumn, Ólafur goes out to search for missing sheep and finds many, quite a few of which belong to chieftain Þorbjörn. Ólafur returns them to the

Political, Economic and Cultural Background

chieftain and becomes involved with a woman on Þorbjörn's farm named Sigríður. The next year the same thing happens. When Ólafur returns the sheep, Þorbjörn is very rude to him.

Because she can expect only harm from Þorbjörn, the chieftain who should be responsible for the people of the district, Þormóður's wife asks Ólafur to drive her dead husband's ghost away from her house. He obliges. To further show his overbearing demeanor, Þorbjörn claims a stranded whale which should be Hávarður's and bullies the arbitrator named to decide the matter into giving it to him. The ghost shows up again and this time Ólafur breaks its back and dumps it into the sea. Every good thing that Ólafur does for people annoys Þorbjörn even more because he sees such services as encroaching on his chieftainly reputation. In the spring Hávarður and Ólafur move to get away from him.

During the summer Þorbjörn goes to the assembly and arranges to marry the daughter of another chieftain, Gestir. This news causes Sigríður to move out, and Ólafur helps her. Irritated beyond words, Þorbjörn, with the help of two others, kills Ólafur and chops out his teeth.

Hávarður is devastated and takes to his bed until the next summer, when his wife, Bjargey, makes him go to Þorbjörn to ask for compensation. When Þorbjörn insults him, he goes home to bed for another year. The next summer, Bjargey makes Hávarður go to the assembly, and with the help of Gestir, he gets an agreement with Þorbjörn, but the chieftain only pretends to settle. As he is counting out the money, he throws Ólafur's teeth in Hávarður's face. This enrages Gestir. Defeated, Hávarður goes home to bed again. Bjargey, who has been supporting the household, now goes out and organizes her relatives to help Hávarður kill Þorbjörn and his supporters. After the killings, the heroes flee to the house of a chieftain called Steinþór for protection.

Meanwhile, two young boys kill another evil man named Ljótur and come to Steinþór for protection. There is feasting and merry-making until Steinþór runs out of supplies and needs to go to Atli, his brother-in-law, to borrow provisions. Atli is a tightwad and hides from his relative so he will not have to share, but his wife gives her brother whatever he wants, then persuades Atli to like it. Atli agrees to behave better and do as his brother-in-law suggests. Steinþór returns home and the games continue until winter passes and it is time to go to the assembly. Then the heroes stay with Atli while Steinþór goes to the assembly to seek a settlement for the killings.

The prosecution falls to Þorbjörn's brother, Þórarinn, who goes with Dýri, an aristocrat in Þórarinn's district, to the assembly to press the lawsuit. Meanwhile Dýri's son, Þórgrímur, and seventeen others start out to sneak up on Atli's farm to ambush the heroes, but Atli discovers the plan in a dream. The heroes are able to plan a defense and defeat the attackers. They spare the lives of three survivors, but shave their heads, smear them with tar, hack off their ears, and send them to the assembly to tell their story.

At the assembly, Gestir is to decide the cases. He matches the killings of one side against those of the other. After he has settled the case, the men with no ears show up and relate what Þórarinn and Dýri had plotted to do. Gestir is angry because of the sneak attack, but allows the rulings to stand. However he promises not to help the attackers in any of their future cases, but to always help Steinþór.

Steinþór then goes to Atli's farm and tells the heroes what has happened. Now everybody goes home. Bjargey is very happy and Hávarður prepares a feast. Steinþór, Gestir, Atli and many relatives come and stay for a week. As they leave, Hávarður gives them all good presents and thanks them for their help. The younger heroes go abroad because they had been sentenced to leave Iceland until Þórarinn, an old man, dies.

Hávarður sells his things and moves north. After some time he hears that King Ólafur Tryggvason has proclaimed Christianity the faith of all Norway, so he, Bjargey, and his kinsman Þórhallur go to Norway and are baptized. Bjargey dies there, but Hávarður and Þórhallur return to Iceland, where Hávarður dies, leaving everything to Þórhallur. He builds a church with the wood Hávarður brought from Norway and has Hávarður buried in the church. Hávarður was thought to be a great man.

POLITICAL ECONOMY, LITERATURE AND THE SOCIAL ORDER OF MEDIEVAL ICELAND

This saga shows a political economy in action, the view of one sagaman who wrote it, and perhaps of a long oral tradition upon which he based his saga, of what life in medieval Iceland was like. The story we derive from interpretations of the literary-historical tradition is that in the last half of the ninth century, when kings in Norway and the British Isles began to consolidate their authority, dissident or disfavored chieftains began to settle in Iceland. They preserved chieftain–follower and owner–slave relationships as the twin bases of the political-economic system when they claimed tracts of land from which they allocated parcels to their free followers. An early and decisive repression of a slave uprising recounted in chapter 7 of *The Book of Settlements* indicates that the new lands were not to be freely available to all who might claim them. Stratification was built in and enforced from the very beginning. The settlers established household economies based on animal husbandry, hunting, and fishing.

Hunting and fishing were important to the economy, as both sagas and archaeological investigations show (Amorosi 1989, McGovern et al. 1988). Grass was the major crop, though there may have been some insignificant grain production. As *Hávarður's Saga* indicates, people kept their livestock indoors during the winter. A household had to control pasture land to produce sufficient hay to feed the sheep and cattle until spring pasturage became available. Hay plays a major part in many sagas, and in this one, a contested meadow is the cause of a killing. Sheep provided meat, as we see from the dramatic description of the autumn meal in chapter 2. Wool was even more important (Ingimundarson 1992), though we see little of it in this saga.

In the summer, people marked their sheep and took them to graze on marginal lands where the grass was too sparse and poor to be harvested. In the autumn, as *Hávarður's Saga* tells, people rounded up all the sheep and separated them, each to their owners. After the round-up, people killed those sheep they did not intend to carry through the winter. They had to match their sheep to the hay they had. The more hay, the larger a herd they could keep.

The amount of hay depended on the amount of land and labor a household controlled. Land without the labor to harvest its hay was useless. But the laborers necessary to harvest the hay required as much in extra provision for their support through the year as the extra hay they could produce would provide. As long as householders had to support laborers through the whole year, as they did slaves, they could not add to their total annual production, and additional tracts of land were of no use to them (Gelsinger 1981). If it was difficult to support productive members of households, it was doubly difficult to support those who produced nothing, as in this saga, when chieftain Steinþór, burdened by a large following, must appeal to his stingy brother-in-law, Atli, for help to support them through the winter.

Icelanders were poor in silver and gold, since they quickly used what precious metals they had to purchase boats and provisions for the trip to Iceland or to import livestock, timber, and iron goods from England or Norway shortly after they arrived (Gelsinger 1981). Raiding expeditions supplied Iceland with some currency, but *vaðmál*, woolen cloth, was the main medium of exchange both within Iceland and with foreign lands.

Icelanders were not merchants in any modern sense. They did not make their living by market manipulations—buying cheap and selling dear. They hoped to benefit by exchanges, but it was a process of social exchange. While they were aware of markets and merchants, such a market-oriented economy did not fit their political system and they demeaned the "market mentality" (Durrenberger et al. 1988). They gave gifts and received other gifts in return. Through such networks of reciprocity they got the timber, grain, weapons, fine clothing, and other imported goods they needed. The more woolen goods they could give away abroad, the more exotic goods they could bring home. The amount of woolen goods a household could produce depended on the number of its sheep and composition of the herd. Wethers (castrated sheep or geldings) and barren sheep yield more wool than ewes. Farmers kept wethers and barren sheep to increase the yield of wool for exchange. To do this, they culled lambs at four to six months of age and kept younger ewes and fed them better. This produced relatively little meat and added to the amount of fodder farmers needed to feed sheep (Ingimundarson 1992). The amount of hay depended on the amount of land and labor.

Cattle were important for dairy products such as milk, a sour cultured-milk product called *skyr*, and cheese. The economic independence of households was defined in terms of the number of cattle they had per dependent. Though cattle defined independence, and sheep indicated wealth, hunting and fishing often provided the food (McGovern et al. 1988). Though cattle play no role in *Hávarður's Saga*, the saga indicates the importance of non-agricultural resources. While Hávarður is in his bed for three years, his wife Bjargey and his kinsman Þormóður row to sea to fish every day. When Bjargey recruits help from her brothers, she uses the metaphors of seal and fishing nets. People had ownership rights over the flotsam that washed up on the tracts of beach they controlled, as we see when Hávarður and Þorbjörn contest the control of a beached whale.

Hávarður's Saga tells us that Þorbjörn Þjóðreksson is a chieftain (*goði*) and Hávarður is his follower (*þingmaður*). In 930 AD Icelandic chieftains founded the general assembly or *Alþing*. This was an annual meeting of chieftains at which they were to hear cases and discuss and modify their customs and usages, *lög*. *Lög* means, literally, "that which is laid down," from the verb *leggja*, which is the causal of the verb *liggja*, which means to lay down. *Lög* is what has been laid down by practice or negotiation. It is much closer to our modern concept of custom than to our concept of law. To translate *lög* as "law" in the modern sense is to suggest a concept and a series of institutions that did not exist in medieval Iceland.

Compared to some sagas, there are few legal cases in *Hávarður's Saga*. Most of the disputes hinge on Þorbjörn's killing of Ólafur. It is typical that none of the disputes receives resolution through law (Miller 1990). First, Hávarður approaches Þorbjörn and requests compensation, only to be insulted with the offer of a broken-down horse. Then, with the support of the powerful chieftain, Gestir, whose daughter had married Þorbjörn, Hávarður approaches Þorbjörn at the general assembly, and Gestir arbitrates a settlement. Not only does Þorbjörn not abide by the settlement, before he is through counting out the money for compensation he again insults Hávarður by throwing trophies of his son's death, Ólafur's teeth, into his face. This so enrages Gestir that he rides immediately away from the assembly to collect his daughter from Þorbjörn's house.

After being twice insulted, Hávarður wreaks vengeance on Þorbjörn. Then Gestir arbitrates a settlement between Þorbjörn's surviving relatives and Hávarður and his followers. None of the cases is resolved through legal procedures. Most cases in medieval Iceland were settled through violence or arbitration rather than through the procedures of the assembly (Miller 1989, 1990). Hávarður, a commoner, can do nothing without the support of chieftains.

Even if one did win a case at the assembly through procedural means, one only won the right to enforce the decision against the defendant himself. If the defendant could muster more force, the plaintiff had no chance of enforcing the verdict. There were no institutional means for enforcing legal decisions, which only legitimized private action (Miller 1990, Jones 1935).

Societies that allow some people privileged access to resources through such concepts as ownership usually develop institutional means for enforcing legal decisions. Anthropologists call such institutional means states (Fried 1967). There was no state in medieval Iceland.

The main function of the general assembly was not to make law nor to adjudicate cases but to make and test coalitions among chieftains. It is at the general assembly that Þorbjörn makes a connection with Gestir by proposing to marry his daughter. Even though Gestir is not enthusiastic about the match, Þorbjörn has enough supporters that Gestir finally allows it. This affinal connection advances Þorbjörn's prestige and power considerably. It is also at the general assembly that Þorbjörn so insults Gestir with his treatment of Hávarður that Gestir dramatically breaks the connection by riding away to claim his daughter back from the overbearing chieftain. It is at the general assembly that Hávarður gains the promise of Steinþór's support.

Every chieftain had followers and every landowner who was not a chieftain had to be a follower of a chieftain. Chieftains formed coalitions among themselves. These were the two important social groups in medieval Iceland: the entourages composed of the followers of chieftains, and the coalitions among chieftains. Both kinds of groups were based on generosity. A chieftain was supposed to support his followers and they were supposed to support him (Durrenberger and Wilcox 1992).

We learn that Þorbjörn was not only an unfair chieftain, he failed to support his followers. In chapter 2, when Þorgerður of Bakki comes to request assistance with her husband's troublesome ghost, Hávarður asks why she does not get Þorbjörn to handle the matter, as he is her chieftain. She says that she "could expect no good there. I would come out well if he did me no evil." Ólafur then attends to the ghost. It is Ólafur who brings missing sheep back to the farmers after the fall round-up. Chapter 2 tells that Þorbjörn's grievance against Ólafur is not so much that he is seducing his housekeeper, Sigríður, but that he is attracting his followers by performing the duties of a chieftain for them. (In *Njal's Saga* this is the explicit motivation for a chieftain whose popularity is on the wane to kill his rival.)

Since the Icelandic economic and political system was based on concepts of ownership, and there were no institutional means for enforcing these claims, everyone had to enforce his own claims to ownership. Chapter 1 of *Hávarður's Saga* tells us of Þorbjörn, "That from some he took away farms or drove them away from their property." One of the major functions of chieftains was to be able to enforce their followers' claims to land, and the followers helped their chieftains amass sufficient force to make good their own and their followers' claims. The larger the coalition of chieftains and the following, the more secure the ownership claims.

A chieftain without followers was powerless, hence chieftains could not afford to lose their followings to others. Chieftain Ljótur, whom the sons of Þorbjörn of Eyrr kill in chapter 14, had so little support that no one did anything about his killing. He had alienated all of his followers by his unfairness. To maintain followers, chieftains had to be generous, as Steinþór is. He is so open-handed that he uses all his household supplies before spring and must replenish his larder from the generosity of his brother-in-law, Atli.

The saga writer illustrates the role of reciprocity and the role of chieftainly support. Hávarður can do nothing without the support of a chieftain. Steinþór offers him a place to stay at the meeting of the general assembly and Gestir supports his case against Þorbjörn in chapter 7. Steinþór offers Hávarður refuge after his rampage, and presents his case, which Gestir again arbitrates at the general assembly in chapter 22. These two chieftains contrast with the two unfair chieftains who do not engage in reciprocal relationships. It is clear from chapter 23 that Steinþór relies on many kinds of connections. He "lacked neither friends nor kinsmen; he was also related by marriage with aristocrats." Chieftain Þórarinn is supported by kinsmen and friends in chapter 19, and it is Þorgrímur, the son of one of his friends, who attacks Hávarður, when he is under the protection of Steinþór's brother-in-law. The saga distinguishes among various kinds of relationships—affinal, consanguineal, and friendship—but all are equally important. Even the distinctions are not absolute.

Frændi meant "kinsman" or "relative." We translate it as "kinsman," and *frændkona* as "kinswoman." Siblings are referred to as or address each other as kinsmen or kinswomen in chapters 7, 8, 14 and 15. In chapter 11 Þorbjörn is a "kinsman" of Vakur, his sister's son, a consanguineal relation. *"Frændi"* is also used as a term of reference and address between Hávarður and Hallgrímur, the son of his sister and his wife's brother, a more distant genealogical connection than sibling. There seems to be a difference between Hallgrímur, with his consanguineal relationship to Hávarður, and his other nephews, related only through the affinal connection with his wife. In chapter 9, Valbrandur, Hávarður's wife's brother, tells his sons that their in-law, *mágur*, has come. Steinþór refers to and addresses his sister's husband Atli as an "in-law" but never as a "kinsman." In chapter 13, however, Hávarður refers to all of his nephews

Political, Economic and Cultural Background 13

collectively, including the affinal ones related only through his wife, as "kinsmen," and elsewhere they are referred to as "companions." It does not appear that *"frændur"* were only consanguineal relatives.

The significant and important relationships in this saga are between in-laws and friends. Atli, Steinþór's brother-in-law, protects his charges and provides Steinþór with provisions when he most needs them. Hávarður's brothers-in-law provide him with their sons to help him gain revenge, though they may be helping their sister as much as him. Steinþór is not related either by blood or marriage, but through ties of friendship, to the people he takes in. Þórarinn and his supporter Dýri are friends, not relatives of any kind. Gestir and Steinþór are friends.

The evidence of this saga suggests that kinship connections were no more important than friendship and affinal relationships; indeed, it suggests that the latter were more important. There is no evidence of any kind of functioning corporate kinship groups larger than families. Bertha Phillpotts (1913) pointed out that settlers did not bring their kinship groups from Norway to Iceland.

The saga writer recognizes and points out the politics of marriage. Þórdís, Steinþór's sister, had been married to Atli for his wealth, as chapter 15 tells us. Þorbjörn married Gestir's sister Þorgerður to benefit from the affinal relationship with the powerful chieftain. He already had one wife, Sigríður, but chapter 1 tells us he could not benefit from her wealth, and she left him when he married Gestir's daughter. While Þorbjörn cannot benefit from either of his affinal relationships, Steinþór benefits from his sister's marriage.

The saga is set in the period after the foundation of the general assembly in 930 AD but before the coming of Christianity in 1000 AD. The year 1000 AD was a turning point in the history of medieval Iceland, not because of the introduction of Christianity but because of the beginning of seasonal labor (Gelsinger 1981). By the year 1000 AD all of the usable land on the island had been claimed. Some people controlled less land than they needed to support their households. They could not produce sufficient hay to keep their livestock through the winters. They had to work for others in return for part of their subsistence. This revolutionized the Icelandic economy.

Slaves were no longer necessary or even useful to increase production. Whereas a slave ate nearly as much as he or she produced in a year, householders could engage a worker for a specific task, and not support him or her through the year. For the first time, there was a source of labor that could produce more than it consumed. Landowners began to free their slaves and replace them with seasonal workers. As they freed slaves, there were more and more people with less than enough land to support themselves, and more people looking for work, and more landowners freed their slaves until slavery disappeared and seasonal work and rental agreements of various types replaced it (Gelsinger 1981).

With the new sources of labor there was no ceiling on the amount of land a landowner could use. Now more land meant more hay, more sheep, and more wool, so there was an incentive to expand production. Since the land was all claimed, the only way to expand production was by taking land away from others as the unjust chieftains Þorbjörn and Ljótur both do in *Hávarður's Saga*.

Thus began a period of turmoil known as the Sturlung age, during which chieftains fought each other with greater and greater ferocity until only a few families remained in control of the island and its land. As the fighting among these families escalated, the suffering of their followers increased.

Meanwhile, other sources of woolen goods were developed in Europe and the price of Icelandic wool fell (Gelsinger 1981). As chieftains in Iceland gained more power, they needed more of the imported goods that symbolized their power—timber, weapons, and grain, which they used especially for brewing for feasts. There were grain shortages in Norway, and angry chieftains often treated visiting Norwegian merchants less than handsomely. Merchants came more infrequently, woolen goods decreased in value, and increasingly fewer chieftains needed more imported goods. Finally one chieftain, Gissur Þorvaldsson, got the others to follow the king of Norway in 1262 AD. Men of the

North and South Quarters agreed to become subjects of the king of Norway and to pay him a tax while the king agreed to preserve tranquility in Iceland, not to introduce new laws without their consent, and to trade with Iceland (Gelsinger 1981).

Most of the Icelandic sagas were written during the chaos of the thirteenth century, but *Hávarður's Saga* was written between 1300 and 1350 AD, some time after Iceland had become part of Norway, and some four hundred years after the events it depicts.

THE STRUCTURE OF *HÁVARÐUR'S SAGA*

Anthropologists have traditionally called societies without states "primitive." The conceptual and cultural systems of medieval Iceland were similar to those of other primitive societies anthropologists have studied as living social orders. When Lin Yeh-hua studied them, the Lolo of Liang Shan in China had feuding aristocrats and commoners, a hierarchic social order and stratification, but no state (Lin Yueh-hua 1961). When Edmund R. Leach lived among them, the Kachin of highland Burma had aristocrats, slaves, feuds, an elaborate system of compensation for wrongs, legal cases, and a tradition of saga telling (Leach 1954). When we were among Lisu in the highlands of northern Thailand, we observed and recorded legal cases, killings, compensation payments, negotiations, marriages, feasts, feuds, divorces, sorcery, ghostly hauntings, and many other kinds of events familiar from the Icelandic sagas (Durrenberger 1992). These are but three of many examples of similar societies to be found in the ethnographic literature.

Claude Lévi-Strauss argues that there are fundamental differences between the mode of thought in such societies and the modern way of thinking. He calls primitive societies "cold" because their conceptual orders are based on a notion of a timeless present. People think of the past and future as the same as the present. Everything—all animals, places, people, events—has a place in an all-embracing classification system Lévi-Strauss calls a totemic operator. Such systems work by a logic of classification and analogy. Individuals are parts of these all-encompassing systems and their places in the system are often indicated by their names.

"Hot," or modern, societies incorporate ideas of historical causality and time into their self-concepts. We explain present realities in terms of cause-and-effect relationships among events, we understand ourselves and our societies in terms of historical processes. The explanations people of "hot" societies accept for events change from one period to another as each generation rewrites history. Understandings of the American revolution have been different for people of the eighteenth, ninteenth, and twentieth centuries as well as for people in the United States, Great Britain, France, Vietnam, and Latin America. The point is not that "hot" societies understand history objectively, but that they explain themselves in terms of some concept of time, origins, causality, and dynamics as opposed to things "having always been this way." Whether "hot" or "cold," the explanations are always cultural artifacts of the people who create them and therefore vary with their cultures.

By the same token, because people think of their society as unchanging does not mean that it does not change. Even though people think of their social order as enduring, it may undergo significant alterations as people argue, disagree, negotiate, and change their culture. People nonetheless think of time as static and conceive of their society as recapitulating itself over and over. To accommodate continued changes, people change their conceptual schemes to match the new realities, all the while maintaining that both the social order and the conceptual system are changeless, "have always been thus." Instead of understanding themselves and their societies in terms of historical processes, primitive, stateless people understand themselves, their societies, and events in terms of their totemic systems. From their point of view there is no history. Time is not dynamic. Events, places, things, animals, people, families are all connected in the totemic operator. People construct explanations and understanding of themselves, others, and their societies in terms of this totemic classification system and logic.

People reinforce these connections not only in action and

in the way they explain events to one another, but also in the stories they tell each other. There is no reason to suppose that medieval Iceland was different from other such societies. Relocating in Iceland may have been an attempt to maintain the system of social relationships and its associated totemic system as it had been in spite of undeniable changes. The formalization of custom (*lög*), the formation of the general assembly, the compromise over Christianity, and the writing of the sagas may have also been attempts to maintain the status quo. Sagas were totemic documents whose cultural function was to attempt to see the changing political, economic, and social realities of the thirteenth century as continuous with a conceptually unchanging model of social relations of the past (Durrenberger 1991).

From at least the year 1000 AD, with the concentration of wealth and power, there were growing pressures on a social system based on stratification without state control. Early Icelanders had a totemic system and developed an ideology of a changeless society. When the changes were significant and undeniable, the need to articulate this ideology was the strongest. The sagas were totemic documents written in an effort to stitch the present to the past, to assert changelessness in the face of change. Sagas are attempts to recreate the totemic structure and to make analogic relationships between the present thirteenth century excesses and the past of, at least, conceived, balanced relationships.

To take one example, *Gunnlaugur's Saga*, one of the sagas of poets, presents the picture of a strongly organized universe with everything in its place and a place for everything, where no human effort or emotion has any power to alter the facts of existence. This is what the saga is and what it is about: the structure of existence, the totemic structure of these people. From his first introduction to his death, Gunnlaugur is haughty, overly concerned with his honor, bragging about his stature and his father's position. Gunnlaugur is the same at the age of twelve, eighteen, and when he dies. Þorsteinn dreams of what will be, and it happens; Önundur and Illugi dream of what has happened, the inevitable consequences happen, and we return to the beginning with the continuation of the recitation of Þorsteinn's genealogy through the children of Helga, his daughter. Simply, this saga says that in spite of all efforts, things turn out as usual, as they must, as they are, as they are laid down. At every juncture, people attempt to change the future. Still, the end is the same as the beginning (Durrenberger and Durrenberger 1992).

Hávarður's Saga may appear to be different. Steinþór's brother-in-law, Atli, changes from a sniveling skinflint of a coward to a formidable warrior and a generous person. Hávarður changes instantaneously from a good-for-nothing bedridden depressed old man to an energetic and athletic champion who inflicts vengeance on all connected with his son's killer.

The saga itself labels these events as unlikely. In chapter 5, "it also seemed not likely to people that any redress would come to his kinsmen because Hávarður seemed to them capable of nothing." In chapter 6, Hávarður's wife, Bjargey says, "There is hope, though it be unlikely, that there would be vengeance for Ólafur ...." Again, in chapter 8, she says to Þórhallur, her and her husband's faithful companion, "It is not likely but it is my thought that there will be vengeance for Ólafur my son." After Hávarður and his nephews have finished their killing rampage and sought refuge, Steinþór says in chapter 13 that, "This has gone more according to circumstance than likelihood." The same chapter reports that the news of Hávarður's exploits spread widely, "and it seemed to most to be a great surprise."

The saga comments on other improbable events. Þorsteinn and Grímur, the sons of Þorbjörn of Eyrr from whom Ljótur tried to take the meadow, kill the unjust chieftain in chapter 14 and take refuge with Steinþór and Hávarður. The puny Atli with his responsibility for the elderly Hávarður, the two boys, and Hávarður's five nephews and two servants defeat the force of eighteen well-equipped fighting men Þórarinn sends against them in chapters 19–21. In this saga, the unlikely happens.

It seems impossible that the feeble Hávarður will be able to get vengeance for his son, but he does. It seems unlikely that the two boys can kill a great champion, but they do. It seems improbable that Atli will defeat and humiliate such a force as is sent against him, but he does. All of these deeds are

Political, Economic and Cultural Background

achieved against great odds in the name of justice against unfair men. The well-structured working out of pattern illustrated in *Gunnlaugur's Saga* is replaced by a hopeful achievement of the improbable in *Hávarður's Saga*.

The probable versus the improbable is but one contrast. In this it differs from other sagas, but *Hávarður's Saga* shares many of the same kinds of structural elements of other sagas in its logic of classification and analogy. The most obvious contrast is the youth of Þorbjörn's sons and the age of Hávarður, each killing an unfair chieftain. The generosity of Steinþór is contrasted with the stinginess of Atli as Atli hides under a haystack until he freezes to avoid having to meet his brother-in-law and face his request for help. The justness of the chieftain Gestir is contrasted with the unfairness of his would-be son-in-law Þorbjörn the chieftain in several contexts, including the scene in chapter 6 in which Þorbjörn insults Hávarður by throwing Ólafur's teeth in his face and spoiling the settlement.

The contrast between those who work and those who do not is repeated in Bjargey's fishing all the while her husband Hávarður is laying in his bed, and in the speech of Steinþór's slave when the refugees ask him to join their games with him in chapter 17. He points out that he will get behind in his work and none of the champions will help him with it. Vakur is introduced in chapter 1 as a person who does not work, in contrast to Brandur, who does. This may be related to a more general contrast between the ridiculous and the normal. The saga holds Hávarður up to ridicule when he pouts. It ridicules Atli's stinginess and Vakur's shouting. It seems normal for young boys, old men, and misers to do what they do when it is the expected thing to do, even though it is unusual or extraordinary for them in their current circumstances.

We see a series of contrasts which we can list as:

stingy	::	generous
not work	::	work
ridiculous	::	normal
just	::	unjust
improbable	::	probable
old	::	young

To this list we can add aristocrat::commoner. The saga describes slaves, servants, dependent kinsmen, independent landowners, and chiefly aristocrats. Slaves are mentioned twice. In chapter 11, after Hávarður and his nephews have killed Þorbjörn and his followers on the beach in front of Þorbjörn's boathouse, Eyjólfur, one of the nephews, asks whether they should kill the slaves. Hávarður says that killing the slaves would not add to his revenge. The second mention comes in chapter 17, when Steinþór asks Svartur, his slave, to wrestle. He does not want to, because he has work to do, and he supposes that none of the wrestlers would help him make up the work he would lose if he stops for their games.

In chapter 4 Þórdís, chieftain Þorbjörn's sister, sends a *skósvein*, literally "shoe boy," to see what is happening when she hears the fight between her kinsman and Ólafur. In chapter 9 when Hávarður is collecting his nephews, Ánn joins the party. He was a "homeman" (*heimamaðr*) and had "house servant's (*húskarls*) work." When Hávarður and his band kill Ljótur, Þorbjörn's brother, in chapter 12, we learn that Ljótur had house servants, *húskarlar*. In chapter 21, Atli assigns his houseservant one man to kill when Þorgrímur Dýrisson of Dýrafjörður attacks his household.

In his first attempt to settle the dispute, Gestir invites Hávarður to come to him, and "he would never treat him like a common worker while they both lived." Clearly there is a class of work that Gestir will not ask Hávarður to do, work suited to common workers or servants. In chapter 2 Vakur chides Ólafur for being a sheep-herder around Ísafjörður. In chapter 4 Ólafur suggests that it is out of place for Þorbjörn to think of herding sheep, as he would be lowering himself or elevating sheep-herders above their places.

Chapter 1 introduces Vakur and Brandur as "*heimamenn*," "homemen," of chieftain Þorbjörn's, who brought provisions to the farm and tended sheep. Vakur was Þorbjörn's sister's son. Chapter 2 introduces the parallel of Þórhallur as a kinsman of Hávarður, a homeman, who took care of his provisions. Ólafur is, of course, Hávarður's son, and tends his sheep. There seems to have been a graduation from slaves to servants to dependent kinsmen, sons, nephews, and others, who worked on the farms gathering provisions, fishing, making hay, and tending to the sheep.

Some people owned farms and were known as *bændur* (sing. *bóndi*), landowners. In this saga Þorbjörn the chieftain, Hávarður, and Steinþór are referred to as *bændur*, even though we know that others such as Ljótur and Þorbjörn of Eyrr, the father of Grímur and Þorsteinn, who are introduced in chapter 14, own land. Among these, some were chieftains (*goðar*, sing. *goði*) who owned a chieftaincy, (*goðorð*). Þorbjörn the chieftain, introduced in chapter 1, for instance, "had a chieftaincy in Ísafjörður." Gestir Oddleifsson, introduced in chapter 4, had many "people managements," another word for chieftaincy. Chapter 19 introduces Þórarinn as a *goðorð-maður*, a chieftaincy-man, or man with a chieftaincy, in Dýrafjörður. All of these are also called aristocrats, *höfðingjar*. This title does not seem to be a synonym for chieftain, as Karlsson (1977) points out. It seems, rather, a title for a more consolidated position, less of the old chieftaincy, more of an aristocrat, one of the few modern thirteenth-century chieftains who has consolidated power rather than one of many earlier chieftains with somewhat equal power.

In modern American parlance, "farmer" is an occupational label, irrespective of tenural status. The semantic range of such terms was different in medieval Iceland. A *bóndi* was a land-owning farmer, a powerful and prestigious position. He was definitely not a peasant. While peasants may own land, they are toward the bottom of the social hierarchies of their societies and definitely not at the top of them. Therefore it is incorrect to translate the term as "peasant." We translate *bóndi* as "landowner" because that is the most important dimension of the title. We translate *búmaður* as "farmer" in chapter 15, where it refers to the practice of husbandry without tenural implications. The distinction of vocabulary shows that the saga author distinguished between "farmer" and "landowner" when he wanted to.

Life at Steinþór's house in chapters 13–15 is the aristocratic life, as compared to Hávarður's life of herding sheep and fishing and Atli's miserly life of hard work. There is joviality, food, and games. Only the slaves work.

In this saga, the title *karl* is used in opposition to *höfðingi*. Chieftain Þorbjörn, Steinþór, Ljótur, Þórarinn, and Dýri are referred to as aristocrats. Interestingly, Gestir, who held many chieftaincies, is not referred to as an aristocrat. Þorbjörn of Rauðssandur and Hávarður are the only ones referred to as commoners, and Þorbjörn only once to Hávarður's fourteen times. Þorbjörn the chieftain, Sigríður, his housekeeper early in the saga, Hávarður, and his wife Bjargey are all referred to as being of great families, *storættaður*. Being of a great family and having land were not sufficient to be a chieftain or an aristocrat. One could own land and be of a great family, like Hávarður, and be a commoner. The number of times Hávarður is referred to or addressed as a commoner suggests that this is an important dimension of contrast. Þorbjörn, his adversary, is referred to seven times by title (three times as an aristocrat, four times as a landowner). His name is mentioned 112 times, so he is mentioned by title about 6% of the time. Hávarður is mentioned by the title of commoner, *karl*, twelve times and landowner once, about 9% of the 138 times he is mentioned. Steinþór is mentioned twice as an aristocrat and four times as a landowner, about 9% of his seventy mentions in the saga. No one else is mentioned more than once by a title.

As it is used in this saga, *karl* is ambiguous. It can also mean "old man." Since age is also a salient dimension of contrast, we translate it as "old man." It can be read equally well as "commoner." In Chapter 7 where Steinþór refers to Hávarður as an "*árftökukarl* " we use the term "client commoner" to convey the sense of dependency suggested by the first part of the term, which indicates a person who gives his wealth to a chieftain in return for support, as well as the commoner status indicated by the second part. Here the term implies helplessness.

The dimensions of social contrast apparent in this saga are freemen vs slaves, house servants and homemen (dependent freemen) vs landowners (independent freemen), commoner vs aristocrat. We can extend the list of oppositions to include these social oppositions:

free	::	slave
landowner	::	dependent
aristocrat	::	commoner

The saga uses the logic of analogy to establish relationships. For instance, Vakur attends his uncle Þorbjörn with idiotic shouting and dies by drowning in inches of water. The noble and generous Steinþór has his witless brother-in-law, Atli. The relationship established is Steinþór : Atli :: Þorbjörn : Vakur. In a contrast reminiscent of that between Flossi and Gissur in *Njal's Saga*, we see the difference between Hávarður and Þorgrímur when Hávarður rejects the suggestion to burn Ljótur in chapter 11, while in chapter 21 Þorgrímur plans to burn Hávarður and his party as the quickest way to achieve his objective. The saga author equates the use of fire with ignominy and the rejection of fire with propriety.

The saga author points out an asymmetry in the episode of the twelve-year-old Þorsteinn and ten-year-old Grímur killing the unfair Ljótur by having Grímur say that he "... is not in a child's reach." This episode balances Hávarður's exploits on the other end of the age continuum. The saga author has Hávarður say that he is no longer fit for such exploits several times. Both are examples of people achieving improbable exploits for their age categories. This logic is echoed when Bjargey recruits her nephews. She does not refer to them directly but metaphorically, as seal nets, fish nets, and turf cutting tools. Each of her brothers offers her everything he has, but points out that one of the implements, the brother, is less than useful for age and wear whereas the others, the nephews, are young and untried.

In a totemic society, magic, spells, dreams, and curses make sense. They are ways of manipulating the classification system, bringing one category into relationship with another. The curses and spells in Icelandic "lay" something else into "that which is laid down," to determine the future. Dreams reveal relationships which are not otherwise apparent. In *Hávarður's Saga* dreams function to reveal the attack on Atli and to provide information to his attackers. Þorgrímur is introduced in chapter 19 as one learned sorcery and magic, but in chapter 21 when Atli's sword does not bite him and Atli accuses him of being troll-like, Þorgrímur points out that Atli seems to be just as invulnerable. In any case, Þorgrímur meets his end not by weapons but because Atli bites through his windpipe. Predictions and curses lay things down in this and other sagas. Thus, when Gestir predicts things in this saga, they are laid down. Gestir also appears as a prescient person with the same power in other sagas such as *Gisli's Saga* and *Laxdæla Saga*.

Magic is at work in the saga. In chapter 8, when Bjargey has Þórhallur row her boat all around chieftain Þorbjörn's, she does something with a bag that infuriates Þorbjörn. Her metaphorical references to her nephews are related to her magic. Her magic transforms Hávarður from a dottering, bedridden old fool into an energetic, athletic, and successful warrior. The saga author even has her say that she needs to use no egging-on words to encourage Hávarður on his way. In terms of the logic of the tenth century, the setting of the saga, Hávarður and his nephews are successful because of Bjargey's magic, which makes the improbable happen. In chapter 6, in a scene reminiscent of Njal's foresight in *Njal's Saga*, Bjargey predicts in detail the events of the assembly Hávarður is about to attend. Prophecies point out the inevitable. The other supernatural aspect of the saga is Ólafur's two fights with the very material ghost of Þormóður.

While other sagas, such as *Gunnlaugur's Saga*, have dense webs of structural oppositions and patterning of events that make outcomes inevitable, in *Hávarður's Saga* the improbable happens rather than the inevitable. Many sagas have dense genealogies, and in some of them, not to have a genealogy is not to have a place, as in *Hænsa-Þórir's Saga* (Durrenberger et al. 1988). *Hávarður's Saga*, in contrast, has only the shallowest of genealogies, extending back only two generations.

We have elsewhere discussed the intricacies of structure in *Gunnlaugur's Saga*, in which the events of the first half of the saga are mirrored in the second (Durrenberger and Durrenberger 1992). *Hávarður's Saga* is only weakly structured in the same way. The first part of the saga outlines Þorbjörn's tyranny (chapters 1–4); the second, Hávarður's helplessness and inability to get compensation from Þorbjörn (chapters 5–8); the third, Hávarður's transformation and killing rampage (chapters 9–21); and the fourth, Hávarður's establishment of balanced social relationships (chapters 22–24). The center of the saga is Hávarður's transformation in chapter 9.

The tyranny of the first section contrasts with the balance of the fourth and the helplessness of the second section contrasts with the effectiveness of the third.

Events do not match in detail throughout the saga, though. Verse 3 might be resigned in contrast to the determination of verse 4, one on either side of Hávarður's transformation in chapter 9. Bjargey's goading of Hávarður at the beginning of the chapter contrasts with her statement that she does not need to egg him on after he arms himself. Hávarður collecting of his nephews for the expedition matches Bjargey's recruitment of them. Þórbjörn's meeting with Bjargey on his way from home in chapter 8 matches his meeting with Hávarður on his way back home in chapter 10. Hávarður's chopping Þórbjörn's teeth from his head in chapter 11 matches Þórbjörn's throwing Ólafur's teeth into Hávarður's face in chapter 7. While such events do seem to form a pattern, the pattern becomes weak or undiscernible farther from the middle of the saga until it is difficult to imagine how more remote events might match each other without forcing them into a pattern that does not seem to fit.

THE IDEOLOGY AND PRACTICE OF HONOUR

The saga author had a clear understanding of both the economics and the politics of chieftainship. The saga portrays the generosity and support of the good chieftain, and the loyalty of his followers. It also points out in no uncertain terms the expenses of such largess and the necessity of having good relations with others to keep the system of reciprocity functioning. The saga author condemns failure of reciprocal relations and contrasts it to successful reciprocity, which he applauds. Twice Ólafur brings the chieftain Þórbjörn's lost sheep back to him, only to meet with ridicule. His only thanks for saving the sheep from the ghostly Þormóður and helping Brandur in chapter 3 is Vakur's scorn. Þórbjörn's taking of Hávarður's whale in the same chapter is what the anthropologist Marshall Sahlins (1972) calls negative reciprocity. In chapter 4 he promises Gestir "to stop unfairness and wrongs, offer that to each person which he has, and hold customs and right ...," but he breaks the promise.

In chapter 14, Ljótur refuses to share an irrigated pasture with its co-owner, Þorbjörn of Eyrr—another failure of reciprocity. The sagaman characterizes each chieftain as an "*ójafnaðarmaður*," an "unfair man," and their actions confirm that they violate all expectations of reciprocity with their followers and fellow chieftains. Atli is also a model of non-reciprocity. He avoids human contact to avoid reciprocal relationships. But, unlike Þorbjörn the chieftain, Atli changes after his wife persuades him and his brother-in-law Steinþór explains things to him.

The saga author describes Þorbjörn the chieftain or his behavior as unfair, *ójafnað*, twelve times in chapters 1, 2, 3, 4, 5, 6, and 22. Ljótur is so described four times in chapters 14 and 22. The sagaman refers to Þorbjörn as *ódrengskapur*, "dishonorable" or "unmanly" (see Foote 1963), three times in chapters 3, 7, and 22. He uses *drengskapur*—"manly" or "honorable"—to describe Þórarinn and Dýri, Þorbjörn's kinsmen, twice in chapter 22—once when they pretend to be honorable and once when Steinþór observes that as a result of their behavior they have lost their manliness. In the same scene Gestir describes Steinþór as having acted *drengiliga*, "honorably" or "manfully." The saga describes the comportment of Hávarður's group in chapter 9 as they weather a hard crossing in a boat, and the fight between Torfi and Sturla in chapter 10, in the same terms. Finally, Hávarður thanks his supporters for their *drengiliga*, "manly," aggression in chapter 23.

Karlmannligur—"manly"—seems to have a similar meaning in similar contexts. Hávarður suggests his son Ólafur try his manhood in a contest against the ghost in chapter 2; Bjargey suggests to Hávarður that it is manly to ask for compensation in chapter 5; the saga describes Hávarður's nephew Hallgrímur as unhandsome looking but manly in chapter 8; Hávarður says much depends on their carrying out their vengeance manfully in chapter 9; Hávarður tells Þórhallur that he shall defend the boat manfully if necessary in chapter 11. In chapter 5 Þorbjörn says Hávarður has lost a manly, *vaskan*, son, and in chapter 9, Bjargey tells Hávarður to act manfully if he wants to avenge Ólafur. In chapter 4 Þórdís,

Þorbjörn's sister, says in a harsh but typical statement to egg her son on to violence that he is loath to commit, "I am a manlier (*vaskari*) daughter than you are a son."

Vaskur meant "manly," *karlmaður* "a man," and *drengur* "a youth," in the sense of a brave, or gallant youth with proper values. We translate *drengskapur* and derived words as "honor, honorable, honorably." We translate the others as "manly" or "manfully" to preserve a sense of the ideology of manfulness as an important dimension of honor. Since there was a well-developed ideology of manhood and manliness, the semantic range is somewhat different from that of modern English. In fact, one of the strongest invectives a woman could use to motivate a man was to question his manhood as Þórdís does when she eggs her son to join the fighting against Ólafur in chapter 4, when she suggests that he is a daughter rather than a son. To accuse a man of femininity was the height of provocation. In chapter 21 Atli is described as *ragi*, which we translate as "womanly" to preserve the meaning of term, and to indicate the contrast with "manly." According to *Grágas*, this term was so insulting that the insulted person could kill or outlaw the person who insulted him.

To be manly was also to follow prevailing custom, that which had been laid down as *lög*. Insofar as practice dictated fairness and equitability, these were aspects of manliness, along with athletic prowess, generosity, trustworthiness, and other virtues. Concepts of fairness did not parallel modern ones, as this saga shows. There is no attempt to fight fairly, with even odds, but rather to achieve surprise and overwhelming force. In this saga, the contrast is between those chieftains, Þorbjörn and Ljótur, who do not conduct themselves according to usage, and those chieftains, Steinþór and Gestir, and commoners, who do. The saga does not suggest that manly comportment is to be expected, or that it is usual, rather the converse, that it is improbable.

Litil, "little," prefixed to *mannliga*, meant "stingy, paltry, mean, unmanly," just as the negating *ó* prefixed to *drengskapur* meant "unmanly," negations of aspects of the ideology of manliness used to insult or describe.

We must be careful, especially in dealing with concepts such as this, not to project our modern prejudices or concepts onto an alien social order and world view. The ideology of manhood was totemic. It was not an ideology of male supremacy or superiority but a totemic concept of keeping everything in its place. Inversions such as femininity in a male were "unnatural," perhaps dangerous, and certainly insulting to suggest. The concept did not rest on power. Þorbjörn and Ljótur both have power, but the saga describes both as being unmanly, and it describes their side in the dispute as losing its manliness after the final settlement. It was not based on wealth, because the wealthy Atli is in the beginning not manly. It was not based on sexual prowess as the first lines of the saga describe Þorbjörn as sexually potent.

When we examine the examples in this saga we see that manliness depends on fairness, generosity, helping friends and dependents in need, honoring agreements, and gaining the esteem of others. These are all characteristics of Steinþór and Gestir. Each of these criteria is abused by Ljótur and Þorbjörn. Both are described as "unfair," as abusive of their dependents, as not honoring agreements, and as held in low esteem by others. Ljótur's fate shows that if one is held in low esteem, there will be no vengeance for him. To avenge a person or get compensation for him is to show one's esteem for him. It is an often mentioned role of women in the family sagas, though they do not wield weapons themselves, to show their regard for their fallen kinsmen by demanding that surviving kinsmen exact vengeance, even at the cost of their own lives.

The depiction of gender relationships raises the same kinds of questions of literary artifice and sociological practice. There are six women in the saga. The first paragraph says that Þorbjörn the chieftain took "daughters of people or their kinswomen and kept them at hand some time and then sent them home." He also took away farms and property. Here Sigríður is introduced as "a young woman and of a great family." Þorbjörn has taken both her and her property. The developing relationship between Sigríður and Ólafur is one of the excuses for Þorbjörn's killing of Ólafur. But it is only one of the ways that Ólafur has assumed chiefly prerogatives. It is Þorbjörn's jealousy over these prerogatives that is the true cause of Ólafur's death. Sigríður is able to get away with her property when Þorbjörn takes a wife at the assembly. She does not egg on Ólafur—on the contrary she tells him to avoid fighting with Þorbjörn. She disappears with Ólafur's death.

Bjargey, wife of Hávarður and mother of Ólafur, is introduced in the second paragraph and plays a major role in the saga. "She was of a good family and the most prominent." She tells Hávarður what to do and carries on with the support of the household while Hávarður is in bed. Bjargey is the sole mover throughout the second quarter of the saga. She is in charge of provisioning the household and of planning what to do. Hávarður only does what she says to do and when she tells him to do it. She is loving and never shames him, but more or less has him go through the proper channels. She makes conditional predictions which come true and she seems to have magic to help realize them. She is rowed around Þorbjörn waving a bag and finds out when Þorbjörn will be returning that way. Then she goes to each of her brothers and asks for the help of her nephews. Next, on the proper day she advises Hávarður to take his nephews and seek vengeance. Then she is not mentioned again until she rejoices on Hávarður's return. Later she goes abroad with her husband, is baptized, and expires. Bjargey's role is the opposite of the familiar egging on one. She is in total control of the action during the second quarter of the saga.

Þorgerður, introduced in the third paragraph, is the wife of Þormóður who becomes a ghost. She asks Hávarður for help to get rid of the ghost when she should have asked Þorbjörn, her chieftain. She is out of the saga after the first ghost fight. Þorbjörn's sister, mentioned in chapter 1 is not named, only indicated in explaining Vakur's relationship to Þorbjörn.

Þórdís is Þorbjörn's other sister and eggs her son on to join the fight against Ólafur. He is killed. "She now became extremely distressed with this story and grieved that she had egged her son on so much. But she still gave them hospitality and nursing." This is the traditional role for women in the sagas—forcing men to take action that they would rather not and tidying up afterwards. In this saga she is the only woman to do so and she regrets it immediately.

A second Þórdís is Steinþor's sister, married to Atli. She is not really introduced, but appears in the third quarter at her home where she asserts her equality by saying, "I think that I decide no less than Atli. I want you to have such as you want." She exercises appropriate hospitality and generosity when her husband will not. She then allows her brother to listen behind the wall hangings while she uses her sexuality to change her husband's opinion of her gift to her brother. Although there is more action at this farm involving the heroes and Atli, Þórdís is never mentioned again.

Gestir's sister, Þorgerður, is married to Þorbjörn through social pressure. When Þorbjörn does not behave as he has promised, she is taken away from him for punishment. She is not named until the divorce and seem not to have been consulted about the marriage or the divorce.

Jochens (1980, 1986) argues the women in the sagas portray the misogyny of Christianity by being agents, like Eve, who bring discord into the otherwise orderly world of men. This would not seem to be so in this saga. Bjargey keeps the household running in an orderly fashion when Hávarður has taken to his bed. It is she who organized the vengeance which restores the balance of social relations. Þórdís, Atli's wife, also maintains proper social relations by giving her brother the food he needs, helping her husband to behave with proper generosity. Out of the six women, only Þorbjörn's sister Þórdís follows the pattern of encouraging men to disorder. Perhaps the feminine roles are as inverted as the masculine ones depicted for the unmanly males.

Clover (1988) argues on comparative evidence with other frontier societies that female infanticide expresses negative feelings towards women and was used as a means of population control, causing women to be scarce and therefore highly valued. She argues that this made for ambivalent feelings about women. However, in medieval Iceland not all the infants who were exposed were female and infanticide in general was a class phenomenon. If there were sufficient resources a family would raise all their children. The poor of the dependent underclass, unable to feed another child, could be forced by their masters to expose children, male or female.

The sagaman does not present women as a monolithic category, but with a good deal of variety in personality and action. There is no question that medieval Icelandic society was heavily male dominated. All women in this saga were women of property, but were introduced by their dependent relationships to men. But numerous men are identified by their dependent relationships to other men. No female slaves or workers are shown as actors. The category of women is not lower than the category of men in regard to power but overlaps it. There were things that women did not do such as fight as warriors or prosecute law cases, but not all men were allowed to do these things either. Power was concentrated in the hands of a few powerful chieftains, all of whom were male. If Sigríður had to have the support of her male kinsman to get herself and her property away from Þorbjörn, Hávarður had to have the support of men more powerful than Þorbjörn to succeed. A very few people had power to control events. Even the highest chieftain could not act alone but had to have the support of his fellow chieftains and his entourage of supporters. Kinship and economic relations wove a web of interrelated ties that encompassed both genders to form entourages of varying degrees of effectiveness. As James C. Scott points out (1991) rulers who fail to adhere to the values they articulate are liable to the criticism that they have broken the social contract they themselves have defined. In medieval Iceland chieftainship was dependent on reciprocity, support, generosity, and fairness, and the other characteristics associated with the ideology of honor. Those voracious chieftains who began to expand their holdings increasingly departed from traditional values. By the time the sagas began to be written in the thirteeenth century, chiefly political action was more commonly expedient and self serving than honorable and reciprocal. The judgments of *Bandamanna saga* are directed at these chieftains (Durrenberger and Wilcox 1992). *Hænsa Þórir's Saga* emphasizes the contrast between the traditional chieftainly values exemplified by Blund-Ketil and the mercantile mentality of Hænsa Þórir. *Hávarður's Saga* is very explicit in its contrast between the overbearing Þorbjörn and the equitable and just Gestir. We have argued that it was just this contrast that motivated the writing of the sagas (Durrenberger and Durrenberger 1992; Durrenberger 1992). The saga is a critique of rapacious chieftains.

SAGA AND HISTORY

When we examine Hávarður's behavior with the ideology of manliness and the dynamics of chieftaincy in mind, we see that it does not change, but goes from where it once was back to the same point. He is described as being of a great family, being a great champion and a great viking. He functions as a chieftain. Followers of Þorbjörn appeal to him for chieftainly help, as chapter 2 self-consciously describes. Because Ólafur is a threat to Þorbjörn's following, Þorbjörn kills him.

If Hávarður acts like a chieftain, he is a chieftain without a following. His absolute lack of power is symbolized in the saga by his going to bed and being inactive. When he does try to get compensation, he receives only insults. After another year of bedridden powerlessness, he attends the general assembly and manages to put together a minimal coalition, an alliance of sorts with two chieftains, Steinþór and Gestir. This coalition is insufficient to gain his ends, and he suffers further insult, but the coalition relationships are sufficient to weaken his opponent, Þorbjörn, since Gestir withdraws from Þorbjörn's coalition.

After a third inactive powerless year in bed, Hávarður, with the help of his wife, and mainly through her kinship connections, manages to put together a minimal following to complement his coalition relationships. With both a coalition and a following, he gains his objective of vengeance and safety. Near the end of the saga he holds a chieftainly feast at which he distributes wealth to those who helped him, just as chieftains do, and at the end of the saga, he brings timber to Iceland and has a church built, the hallmark of chieftaincy. While Hávarður never has chieftainly office or title, he acts like a chieftain. He puts together the elements of chieftaincy, and finally has the status markers of chieftaincy. Bjargey's magic does not achieve the improbable, but assists categories of a totemic system to achieve their proper alignments and mutual balances, their proper totemic order which unmanly chieftains have disrupted.

Likewise, Atli does not change, but resumes his position. Chapter 15 describes him as the least of men, but says he was from larger people. By the end of chapter 22, Atli is thought the best of men. He won this esteem by his loyalty, his adhering to his promise to protect Hávarður and his followers, his generosity, and only partially because of his ferocity. His fierce fighting was but a means to the end of adhering to a promise in the aid of fairness. The initial Atli is the aberration, the one who, for his character's fault, was stingy and anti-social. He returns to the esteemed position of his forbearers by his proper, manly, conduct.

In his last days, Hávarður should be inactive. His brothers-in-law are "retired." His nephews are just on the verge of adult status. Þorsteinn and Grímur, the young boys who kill Ljótur, are too young, as Hávarður is too old, for the manly role of warrior they take on. All of them are commoners, not aristocrats. The proper, manly, totemic, order of events would have been for Þorbjörn to have found the lost sheep of his followers, for Þorbjörn to have dealt with the ghost that troubled his followers, and for Þorbjörn to be generous with his followers, and keep to his agreement with Gestir to uphold the customs and usages and be fair. And so for Ljótur of Rauðasandur, whom the two boys killed. The saga represents the aristocratic disruptions of order as probable and the restoration of order by old men and boys to be improbable.

In his 1943 introduction to the *Íslenzk Fornrit* edition of the saga, Guðni Jónsson points out that the saga confuses many personal and place names, that it contains many inaccuracies and impossibilities if we are to believe other sources such as the *Book of Settlements, Landnámabók*. But *Landnámabók* mentions the saga as the *Saga of Þorbjörn and Hávarður the Cripple* or the *Saga of the Ísfirðings*, the people of the Icefjord. The internal evidence of the saga, such as the mention of the lawman, suggests the late date of composition. Guðni Jónsson concluded that the saga we know as *Hávarður's Saga* is not the same work as the one referred to in the earlier *Landnámabók*. This is a reasonable conclusion, especially since a saga need not have been written.

Hávarður's Saga mentions in chapter 23 that in accordance with Gestir's settlement, the nephews go abroad to plunder and become famous until Þórarinn died, and that there are many sagas of them in Iceland. There is no evidence that these sagas were written. The *Saga of Hávarður* could have been an oral artifact for a long time before a sagaman inscribed some version of it. Whatever liberties the sagaman took with the materials he had to work with, however he changed or perverted them, he produced a cultural artifact of his own period. He could do nothing else. Thus the dating of an inscription of a saga by internal evidence does not date the saga itself.

The saga should tell us something about the period of its composition or inscription as well as the period it was about. We do not claim that all of the events occurred just as they are recorded in the saga, that all of the dialogue was spoken as it is recorded, or even that all of the people existed. Such questions are irrelevant to the cultural and sociological interpretation of the saga. The interesting questions are whether there were chieftains and followers, how the coalitions of chieftains worked, and how relations between chieftains and followers were structured. Looking back on the period from the mid fourteenth century, the sagaman might project his own realities onto the past. Aristocrats replace chieftains. Aristocrats cannot be counted on to treat their followers well. Other aristocrats may be fair, but fairness is improbable. Force rules. Justice is improbable. Reciprocal relationships are in doubt.

An often mentioned difference between the earlier period and Sturlung and later times was the difference between paganism and Christianity, as this and other sagamen point out. The sagaman recognizes another difference when he describes Hávarður claiming unclaimed land at the end of chapter 3. There were continuities and differences between earlier times and Sturlung times. If the values of some of the variables in the social order had changed, the social and political system was still composed of the same variables (Byock 1982).

The Sturlung chieftains were fewer, more powerful, and more rapacious, and perhaps more violent, but they were chieftains and there were still followers and assemblies and coalitions of chieftains, the same kinds of social and political units that the first settlers had brought with them to Iceland, if in different ratios. In the fourteenth century, when *Hávarður's Saga* was written, there was a different system, composed of different relationships among different elements. In this state system, reciprocity was no longer a major organizing principle (Durrenberger 1982).

If the sagaman recognizes aspects of the tenth century system, he also projects elements of his own period onto the past. Þorkell, the intimidated lawman who grants the whale to Þorbjörn in chapter 3 is from a different system of governance, a state system organized into territorial units with appointed officials. Vígfusson and Powell (1905:240) even name an Orm Sturlason, a sixteenth century lawman, as the prototype of Lawman Þorkell. They say that "he was notorious for readiness to oblige those in power ... awarded the same thing to both claimants, quashed his own sentences, and was ready to give any decision required of him."

While there had always been landowners and dependents, chieftains and non-chieftains, the great differences of life-style between aristocrats and commoners portrayed in this saga probably developed as chieftains began to concentrate wealth and power after 1000. It is improbable that any Icelandic household of the tenth century could support sixty unproductive men, as Steinþór's does. To be able to support such a following indicates access to wealth beyond the means of early chieftains. Access to such wealth would only come with the concentration of land and power of later periods.

Even in Sturling times, it was not routine to keep such a following. It would strain any chieftain's productive followers to contribute to such support. Such followings are more characteristic of state systems with broader bases of support than Icelandic chieftains had, systems based on taxation. Travel to Norway was routine in the tenth century, but waned in the Sturlung and later periods. The lack of overseas travel, the great distinction between commoners and aristocrats, and the territorial lawman are projections of a later system onto the tenth century.

By this time, change is undeniable, even by cultural manipulation. If the sagas of the thirteenth century were attempts to deny change by stitching the present to a conceptually unchanging past through a totemic logic, the effort had failed by the fourteenth century, and Icelanders found themselves in a new and different system, a new and different period of time. Thus the sagaman does not lock past, present, and future together into one crystalline totemic structure as in *Gunnlaugur's Saga*, but breaks it down. The saga does not return to the beginning, to recapitulate the system again and again, but points to a different system with the coming of Christianity and the building of the church in which Hávarður is buried. Magic restores the totemic order, but the restoration of the totemic order is self-consciously improbable. The improbable happens through the medium of magic.

TRANSLATION ISSUES

Throughout the introduction, translation issues have been implicit. We have suggested reasons for translating terms such as "landowner," "aristocrat," "homeman," and others in the way we have. At issue in these terms is much more than matters of taste or aesthetics. Often, as with "farmer," the issue is sociological. There are less obvious examples such as "wealth" rather than "money" because there was no market economy and money did not change hands much but wealth did. Compensation payments and other transactions were often in terms of wealth in the form of woolen goods and livestock, not what modern people speak of as money. To use the word "money" where the text uses "wealth" suggests a modern market economy.

In our 1992 book we developed a detailed discussion of translation issues that arose from comparisons of translations of *Gunnlaugur's Saga*. These include time sense, equality of emphasis within sentences, and formulaic expressions. We argued that a translation should be as close as possible to the Icelandic to preserve the shifting tenses, the lack of dependent clauses and resulting equality of emphasis, and the repetitive formulaic expressions that introduce new chapters and characters.

The problem is how to achieve a translation that reflects the original and is still intelligible to a modern reader of English. Shakespeare wrote in English, but is largely unintelligible to modern readers because of radical differences in the social and ideological system of his day and ours. While we can read the words and sentences, we cannot understand the social relations and ideas without the aid of copious scholarship to help us comprehend the differences and appreciate Shakespeare's world in its own terms insofar as we can understand any different culture in its own terms. Thus, modern Icelandic is not a very good guide to medieval Icelandic, and modern Icelanders are not privileged in their access to the literary-historical tradition any more than the English are to Shakespeare. In fact, the fewer assumptions we bring to such studies, the better. The anthropological warning against ethnocentrism is just as relevant for historical inquiries as for contemporary ones.

One solution is not to translate, to simply suggest that if you want to read sagas, you should learn medieval Icelandic. This is one approach, and it has much to recommend it. One problem is that as with Shakespeare, the issues are not just linguistic. Knowing the language is no guarantee of appropriate interpretation. Another problem is that if you would like to sample a variety of the world's cultures, literatures, and histories, you are not likely to be able to learn all of the relevant languages. It would be nice if we all read Arabic, Chinese, Hebrew, Burmese, Aramaic, Linear B, Mayan Glyphs, Pali, Japanese, Urdu, Sanscrit, Swahili, Thai, Tibetan, Mongolian, Lao, Na Khi, and other important languages, but it takes much time and study to understand another language. When you want to learn something of Tibet's Book of the Dead, you don't expect to be told to learn Tibetan; if you want to read the I-Ching, you don't have to learn Chinese.

So we translate. The problem is how to bring the subtleties of haiku from Japanese into English when the very structure of the languages is so different. And so for any translation. Some argue that it is best to try to convey the sense of the story or poem and make the translation as artistic as possible by some cannons of literary beauty. So some saga translators try to make Icelandic sagas approximate modern novels, nineteenth- or twentieth-century artifacts. Others intentionally try to alienate the saga from the reader by using purposefully archaic language to suggest a time of long ago. We have not smoothed out the rough edges of this saga, but we have tried to leave them as we found them. We have no interest or stake in trying to improve this artifact any more than we would a work in an art museum. Rather, we wish to convey as closely as we can, a sense of the artifact. We therefore try to neither to convert the saga into a novel nor to make it seem romantically archaic.

There are two previous translations of *Hávarður's Saga*: Magnússon's and Morris's of 1891 in Volume 1 of their *Saga Library*, and Vígfusson's and Powell's 1905 rendition in their *Origines Islandicæ*. In their introduction, Vígfusson and Powell suggest the saga must be a degenerated sixteenth-century collage of mistakes, copies of parts of other sagas, and inventions of copiests to fill in blanks in their manuscripts. Vígfusson and Powell have a concept of what the saga should naturally be, and to the extent that the manuscripts depart from that model, they judge them faulty. They judge Gestir's final arbitration of the case to be "preposterous," and everything beyond chapter 10 as absurd or "monstrously improbable." Vígfusson and Powell take it upon themselves to eliminate what they see as the absurdities of the saga. They delete the contributions of their imagined scribe to what they see as the final degenerate patchwork of the saga. While they think some scribes were imaginative and creative enough to fill in gaps, and contribute alterations here and there, some others must have been considerably less creative, as they produced a number of identical paper copies. Rather than taking this as evidence that the saga had coherence for its audience, enough to be recognized and copied for some reason, Vígfusson and Powell follow the tradition of their imaginary creative scribe and change the text to make it fit their preconceived notions of what a proper saga should be.

Magnússon and Morris have more respect for the text and at least translate all of it, including verses, even though their translations are often fanciful. In chapter 4, chieftain Þorbjörn and Vakur meet Ólafur and intend to kill him. Ólafur is herding some sheep. Þorbjörn suggests the three walk together. Ólafur answers:

> Ekki er þat samfært, af því at ek verð at reka heim fá mitt; væri þat sanntalat, at þá stækkisk sauðrekarnir um Ísafjörð, ef þú lægðir þik svá. (28 words)

Political, Economic and Cultural Background

We translate this passage as:

> That will not work because I must herd my sheep home. It would be truly said that the sheepherders in Ísafjörður are becoming greater, if you lower yourself so. (29 words)

Magnússon and Morris render the same passage as:

> It falleth amiss, because I must needs drive my sheep home; and verily it might well be said that sheep-drovers shall be getting great men in Icefjord if thou shouldst lower thyself so far as to take to that craft. (40 words).

Vígfusson and Powell give the passage as:

> Our ways lie apart, for I am bound to drive my sheep home, and it would be a true tale that the 'drovers in Icefjord are big men' if thou were to come with me. (35 words)

While Magnússon and Morris, in their inimitable way, manage to convey something of the meaning of the passage, they also obfuscate it, suggesting that shepherding was a craft to which one could take rather than a lowly job fit for slaves and dependents. They expand the passage by twelve words, more than forty percent. Vígfusson and Powell expand the passage by a more parsimonious twenty-five percent, but do not preserve the important sociological concept that Þorbjörn would be lowering himself were he to herd sheep. One cannot demand a word for word translation because sometimes it takes more than one English word to translate an Icelandic word, and sometimes several Icelandic words translate as a single English one. Both of these translators have transformed the text more than the requirements of translation demand. Magnússon's and Morris's translation is only loosely related to the Icelandic text. Others have criticized this style of translation as neither preserving the original sense of the text nor providing an intelligible English text, and we have argued that close translations such as ours best preserve integrity of the sagas as cultural artifacts (Durrenberger and Durrenberger 1986, 1992).

Of the two, Vígfusson and Powell provide a closer translation, though it is not always very close to the Icelandic text. The main fault of their translation is that they have arbitrarily omitted greater and smaller segments of the text to make it fit their preconceived ideas of what the saga should be. Such gaps severely distort the saga as a whole and obliterate such structural patterns as we have discussed. In addition, instead of presenting the saga as it is, even where it does not match other sources, they take it upon themselves to correct it. Where names do not match those of *Landnámabók*, the translators change them in an attempt to correct the saga's "historical" as well as its "literary" faults. Given such a policy of correction, the resulting document cannot preserve much of the Icelandic saga it was modeled after.

Sagas are not novels. They follow different patterns of relevance, selection, logic, character, classification, and presentation. To make sagas familiar to a modern audience, one would try to translate sagas as novels. This practice would entail significant transformations of the cultural content of the sagas (Durrenberger and Durrenberger 1986, 1992). To appreciate cultural differences, readers must be able to perceive the contrasts with what is familiar to them, then question the differences, and then try to understand them. Whatever the difficulties of translating haiku from Japanese, one does not try to transform them into other poetic forms. We try to make the perception of difference possible by preserving rather than smoothing over differences between the saga and more modern forms.

In our translation we have tried to retain something of the original metaphoric structure, though it is impossible to preserve it fully. When the saga says, as others do, that a man had or got a woman it means that he married her, but we preserve the original sense in order to indicate something of the conceptual structure as well as the social relationship. The verb "*eiga*" has all of the ambiguities of the English counterpart, "have" as in "to have a sister, wife, father, farm, friend, problem, or alliance." We therefore preserve its sense with the English, "have." We translate *karl* as "old man" to emphasize the dimension of age rather than as "commoner" to emphasize the dimension of class.

The translation of Old Icelandic poetry poses special problems. The verses are intricate weavings of metaphoric reference with sound patterns. Even the contemporary

Icelanders needed the guidance of Snorri Sturlason's manual to sort out verses and today there is an extensive literature on Old Iceland verse. We cannot pretend to have done more than preserve some of the semantic content of the verses.

Modern readers may well find the reading rough and strange. They may find themselves slowing down, rereading, puzzling over unfamiliar constructions and concepts. If so, we have succeeded. We have attempted to stay as close to the Icelandic as we could within the confines of the English language in order to preserve a sense of difference. In a different cultural world one must expect different customs.

We have by and large followed the edition of the saga presented in Bragi Halldórsson, Jón Torfason, Sverir Tómasson, and Örnólfur Thorsson's volume 2 published by Svart á Hvítu in 1987, though we have also used the *Íslenzk Fornrit* edition from which we have extracted the quotation in this essay.

The Saga of Hávarður of Ísafjörður

CHAPTER 1

It is the beginning of this saga that a man was called Þorbjörn. He was Þjóðrekur's son. He lived in Ísafjörður on the farm which is called Laugaból. He had a chieftaincy around Ísafjörður. He was a man of great family and a great aristocrat and the most unfair man, so that no people there around Ísafjörður had strength to speak against him in anything. He took daughters of people or their kinswomen and kept them at hand some time and then sent them home. He took away the farms from some or drove them away from their property. Þorbjörn had taken that woman for his farm who was called Sigríður. She was a young woman and of a great family. She had much wealth, and it should remain for her and not go out, while she would be with Þorbjörn.

A man was named Hávarður. He lived at a place which is called Blámýrar. He was a man of great family and was then in the decline of age. He had been a great viking in the early part of his life and the greatest champion, and in one fight he had been severely wounded and got a wound under the kneecap, and from then on he always limped. Hávarður was married, and his wife was called Bjargey. She was of a good family and the most prominent. They had one son, who was called Ólafur. He was young and the most accomplished of men. He was big, handsome looking. Hávarður and Bjargey loved Ólafur greatly. He was obedient to them and also tractable.

A man was called Þormóður. He lived at the farm which is called Bakki in Ísafjörður. His wife was called Þorgerður. Þormóður was unpopular with everyone. He was then somewhat in the decline of age. It was said that he was not single-shaped.* It also seemed to every one of them he was the worst to deal with.

A man was called Ljótur, who lived at Mánaberg in Ísafjörður. Ljótur was a big man and strong. He was a brother of Þorbjörn's and was most like him in all ways.

A man was called Þorkell, who lived on the island which is called Æðey. He was a wise man but still a little man, even though of a good family and he was the most insincere of men. Þorkell was the Ísafjörðurs' lawman.

Two men are named to the saga. One was called Brandur, and the other Vakur. They were homemen** of Þorbjörn of Laugaból. Brandur was big and powerful. It was Brandur's work, that he took trips in summers and brought what was needed to the farm, but in winters tended old sheep. He was popular and undemanding. Vakur was Þorbjörn's sister's son. He was a little man and insignificant, argumentative and foul mouthed, he always urged his kinsman Þorbjörn to that which was worse than before. Vakur became unpopular from it, and people told it as it was about him. He worked at nothing but went in and out with Þorbjörn and also went on his errands when Þorbjörn wanted to have evil work done.

A woman was called Þórdís, who lived at Hváll in Ísafjörður. She was a sister of Þorbjörn's and Vakur's mother. She also had another son, who was called Skarfur. He was both big and strong. He was with his mother and looked after their farm.

A man was called Þórálfur, who lived at a place which is

---

*Sagas often refer to "shape changers," or individuals who were not "single-shaped" as this saga puts it. This was one of several categories of people with greater than normal powers.

**Homemen were people who did not have sufficient means to support themselves and therefore attached themselves to a household in return for support. They were often relatives, and somewhat higher in status than servants.

called Lónseyri. He was a popular man and not powerful. He was closely related to Þorbjörn's housekeeper. Þorálfur had offered to take Sigríður in and lend out her money for interest, but Þorbjörn did not want that and showed there again his unfairness and told him he had no say in this.

CHAPTER 2

There is now to take up the story, that Ólafur grows up at Blámýrar. He becomes a promising man. People say that Ólafur Hávarður's son has a bear's warmth, because it was never so frosty or cold that Ólafur wore more clothes than a shirt belted in his britches. He never went away from the farm with more clothes.

A man was called Þórhallur. He was a kinsman of Hávarður's and a homeman, a young man and the most energetic. He supplied provisions to their household.

It was one fall that the Ísafjörðers walked their common pastures, and people rounded up little. Þorbjörn of Laugaból was missing sixty geldings. Winter nights passed, and they were not found.

A bit before winter Ólafur Hávarður's son leaves from home and walks the common pastures, all mountains, looks for people's sheep and finds many sheep, both those Þorbjörn had and theirs, father-and-son,* and also other people's, then he herds the sheep home and brought to each those he had. Ólafur becomes popular from this, so that everyone wished him well.

One day early Ólafur herds Þorbjörn's geldings down to Laugaból. He came at that time when people sat at table and no people were outside. Ólafur knocks on the door, and a woman went to the door. It was Sigríður, Þorbjörn's housekeeper, and she greeted him well. She asked, what he wanted.

---

*The Icelandic word *"feðgar"* denotes the collective unit of father and son.

Ólafur answers: "I have herded Þorbjörn's geldings here, which were missing to him in the fall."

And when Þorbjörn heard that there was a knocking at the door, he asked Vakur to find out what had happened. He did so and went to the self-slamming door. He saw then, that Sigríður and Ólafur were talking together. Then he leapt up on the door-brace and stood there while they talked.

Then Ólafur said: "Now I do not need to go farther. Now you, Sigríður, shall tell about the geldings."

She says that it shall be so, and bid him farewell. Vakur leapt into the hall shouting. Þorbjörn asked why he behaved so and what had happened.

"I think," he said, "that Ólafur the idiot of Blámyrar, son of Hávarður, came. He has herded your geldings here, those which were missing in the fall."

"That was well done," says Þorbjörn.

"I think there has been something more behind the journey," says Vakur, "because Sigríður and he have talked all morning. I saw that it seemed very good to her to lay her arms around his neck."

Þorbjörn said: "Although Ólafur is a hearty man, it is overbold of him to go on unfriendly journeys to us."

Ólafur goes home. The seasons pass, and it is said that Ólafur always comes to Laugaból and met Sigríður, and they got on well together. It was soon talked about, that Ólafur seduced Sigríður.

And next fall people walked their common pastures again and round up little. Þorbjörn was again missing the most. And when the distribution was finished, Ólafur goes from home by himself and walks the common pastures extensively over the mountains and heaths, again finds many sheep and herds them into the settlement, again brings to each that which he has. He now became so popular with the settlement people, that all wished him well except Þorbjörn. He is furious with him for everything that others praise him for, and that which he hears said around the settlement about Ólafur's travels there to meetings with Sigríður. Now Vakur does not hold back from slandering them to Þorbjörn.

Now it so happens, that Ólafur has come to Laugaból with the geldings, as many as before, and when he came, no people were outside. Now he walks inside and into the hall. Landowner Þorbjörn was there in the hall and his kinsman, Vakur, and many of his homemen. Ólafur walks farther inward on the floor. He holds his ax in front of him. And when he comes farther in almost to the dais, he sticks the ax shaft down and leans on it, but no one greeted him, and all were silent. And when he sees, that no one mutters to him, then he says a verse:

Verse 1

> I might first advise it,
> to ask the least wordy freemen,
> Why all are silent here,
> well-spoken shield's warriors?
> Men give no valuation
> to wordless gallants.
> I have stood here long,
> I have been greeted by no one at all.

Then Ólafur said: "It is my errand here, landowner Þorbjörn, that I have herded your geldings here."

Then Vakur said: "It is now known to people, Ólafur, that you have become a sheepherder around Ísafjörður. We also know your errand here, that you start claiming a share of the sheep. That is also the beggar's share, and of course we remember it, although it be little."

Ólafur answers: "That is not my errand. I shall not herd the third time."

He then turns away, but Vakur leaps up and shouts at him. Ólafur paid no attention to it and went home, and the seasons pass. And in the fall people round up well except Þorbjörn. He was missing sixty geldings and they were not found. Those kinsmen, Þorbjörn and Vakur, let the word go around, that Ólafur again intended to claim a share or else steal them.

It was one evening, when they, father-and-son, sat at table and on the dish in front of them lay a leg of mutton.

Ólafur took it up and said, "This is a surprisingly large and fat leg."

Hávarður said, "I think though, kinsman, that it is from our sheep, and not landowner Þorbjörn's, and it is much to endure such unfairness."

Ólafur lays down the leg on the table and reddened, and it seemed to them, who sat there, that he thrust against the table, but still the mutton leg broke in two and so quickly, that one part flew into the wall, so that it was stuck. Hávarður looked up and said nothing, but smiled though.

And just then a woman walked into the hall, and Þorgerður of Bakki had come. Hávarður welcomed her well and asked the news.

She tells of Þormóður's expiration, her husband. "It is not, though, well with us, because he visits his bed every night. Therefore I would accept some help from you, landowner, because my people found Þormóður hard to deal with, but now it is so, that all are thinking of leaving."

Hávarður answers: "I am now out of my most active age and not capable of such, but why do you not go to Laugaból? It is to be hoped of aristocrats, that they would have quickly sent help for such in their local jurisdictions."

She answers: "I do not expect anything good from there. I am pleased if he does me no evil."

Then Hávarður spoke: "It is my advice that you ask Ólafur, my son, and it would be for young men to test their manliness so. In the old days we would have thought it a game."

She now does so. Ólafur promised the journey and asked her to stay there for the night, and the next day, Ólafur went home with Þorgerður. All the folk there were uncheerful, and in the evening people went to sleep.

Ólafur lay in a gable bed out by the door. A light burned in the hall. It was light above, but dark below. Ólafur lay down in a shirt and britches, because he never wore more. He threw a cloak on himself. And when it was nightfall, Þormóður walked into the hall and swung his head. He saw that the bed was occupied, which was not usual. He was not very hospitable, he turns to it and grabs the cloak. Ólafur does not want to let loose and holds until they divide the cloak between themselves. And when Þormóður finds there is strength in the one who is there, he leaps up into the bed. Ólafur leapt up and grabbed the ax and had intended to strike him, but things happened too quickly, Þormóður grabbed him. Then Ólafur had to respond. The hardest fight began. Þormóður grabbed so hard that all the flesh squeezed out from under where he grabbed. Also most things in their way were torn loose, and just then the light went out. Ólafur thought that that did not improve things. Þormóður attacked eagerly, and eventually it happens that they go outside. In the field lay a great drift log, and it so happens, that Þormóður catches both his heels on the log and falls backwards. Ólafur then lets his knee follow the belly, there plays there with Þormóður, until he can arrange what is fitting for him. All the people were quiet when Ólafur walked in. And when he let them hear him, it was all at once, that the light came on and the people were up and rubbed him high and low. He was maimed everywhere from Þormóður's attack. Each man's child who could speak thanked him. He says that he thinks they will not be harmed by Þormóður.

Ólafur stayed there some nights, and then went home to Blámýrar. From this work he became famous widely in Ísafjörður and all quarters* of the land, and from all this the dislike between him and Þorbjörn grew greater.

---

*In the sixth decade of the tenth century, Iceland was divided into four quarters. There were nine chieftains in each quarter except the Northern which had twelve (Byock 1988:65–66).

CHAPTER 3

There is this to tell next, that a whale comes to Ísafjörður, where Þorbjörn and Hávarður had driftage on two sides. It was said at once, that Hávarður should have it. That was the best red whale. Both went there and intended to have a decision of a lawman on it. A crowd of people gathered there. It seemed apparent to all, that Hávarður would have the whale. Lawman Þorkell had come there. He was then asked who should have it.

Þorkell answered, and rather low: "Certainly, they have a whale," he said.

Then Þorbjörn went at him with his sword drawn and said: "Which then, wretch?" he says.

Þorkell answered quickly and drooped his head down: "You, you certainly," he says.

Þorbjörn then went to it with his unfairness and took all the whale. Hávarður went home and was ill content with his part. It seemed to all people Þorbjörn had now again shown his unfairness and complete lack of honor.

It was one day that Ólafur goes to his sheep house because the weather was hard in the winter, and people much needed to take care of their sheep. The weather had been hard during the night. And when he intended to go home he sees that a man walks to the house. Brandur the strong has come there. Ólafur received him well. Brandur took his greeting well. Ólafur asked why he came so late.

He answers: "It is not much to tell. I went to my sheep early today but they had been let to wander down on the beach. There one may herd them up from the beach in two places. But always as I tried there stood a man there in front and waved in front of the sheep so that they leapt back to my arms and it has gone so all day until now. Now I want eagerly that we both go together."

"I want to do as you request."

Then both go down to the shore. And as soon as they want

The Saga of Hávarður of Ísafjörður

to herd the sheep up they see that Þormóður is there in front, Ólafur's wrestling companion, and he waves at the sheep so that the sheep leap back to them.

Then said Ólafur: "Which do you prefer, Brandur, to herd the sheep or to attack against Þormóður?"

Brandur answers: "I will choose the easier, to herd sheep."

Ólafur goes there opposite where Þormóður stood above. There was much snow lying in front of the ridge. Then Ólafur ran at once up on the ridge at Þormóður, but he gives him space. And when Ólafur comes up Þormóður immediately grabs him. Ólafur also responds according to his strength. They go at it a long time. It seems to Ólafur that Þormóður has not slackened after the beating. It happens that they both fall at once towards the edge of the ridge and when it happened so, they roll each other until they both tumble down the snow pile. Then they are alternately under until they come to the beach. Then it so happened that Þormóður was on the bottom. Ólafur takes advantage of this and broke his back in two, prepared him as he liked and swam out in the sea with him long from land and sank him down in the depths. Since then it always seems haunted if people sail near there. Ólafur swam to land. Then Brandur had brought up all the sheep and welcomed Ólafur well. Then they both went home.

And when Brandur came home it was late at night. Þorbjörn asked what had kept him. Brandur told what had happened and how Ólafur had stood to for him.

Then Vakur said: "You have become afraid when you praise that idiot. His greatest distinction will be that he fights ghosts."

Brandur answers: "You would have been more afraid, because you are mostly talk like foxes are mostly tails; and you may in no way compare yourself with him."

They talked there until they were both displeased.

Þorbjörn asked Brandur not to take up common interests with Ólafur. "It will not do for you or any other to put Ólafur in front of me or my kinsmen."

Now the winter passes.

And when it becomes spring they talk together, father-and-son, Hávarður and Ólafur.

Hávarður said: "It so happens kinsman that I have no disposition to live longer so near to Þorbjörn because we have no power to hold our own with him."

Ólafur answers, "It is little to me to have it as compensation to flee in front of Þorbjörn, but I want you to decide. But where do you want to look then?"

Hávarður answers: "Out on the other side of the fjord are many ruins and open land which no person has. I want to go there to raise us a farm and there we will be near our kinsmen and friends."

They take up that plan, move all their livestock and goods which they have and build there the best farm. From then on it is called Hávarðsstaðir. At this time they were the only landowners in Ísafjörður, who were settlers.*

CHAPTER 4

Þorbjörn Þjóðrekur's son rode each summer to assembly with his men. He was a great aristocrat, of a great family with many kinsmen.

At that time Gestir Oddleifur's son lived at Hagi in Barðaströnd. He was a great sage, wise and popular and the most foresightful of men and had many domains.

The same summer when they, father-and-son, would move their dwelling-place Þorbjörn rode to assembly and began his courtship and asked a sister of Gestir Oddleifur's son. Gestir took this matter slowly and said he thought little of Þorbjörn because of his unfairness and overbearingness. But because

---

*The Icelandic "*landnámsmenn*," from "*landnám*" which meant the taking possession of land by occupying it. The term "settler" usually refers to the original settlers of Iceland rather than internal settlers as here.

The Saga of Hávarður of Ísafjörður

there were many helpers for the matter with Þorbjörn Gestir gave a choice that this marriage should hold if Þorbjörn promised him with a handshake to stop unfairness and wrongs, let each person keep which he has and hold customs and right. But if he would not go for this then should Gestir revoke the courtship and make their separation. Þorbjörn agrees to this and they transact it as so spoken. Then Þorbjörn rode with Gestir from the assembly home to Barðaströnd and this wedding took place there in the summer. There was the best feast.

And when this news was reported in Ísafjörður Sigríður and Þórálfur, her kinsman, take the decision to summon landowners and let them value for Sigríður all her wealth from Laugaból. She went to Þórálfur at Lónseyri. And when Þorbjörn came home to Laugaból he became greatly angry, that Sigríður was away, promised Sigríður and Þórálfur hard conditions and anger towards the landowners, who had valued her wealth, then Þorbjörn immediately becomes the hardest to deal with. It seemed to him he has grown even greater from this marriage connection.

The sheep of landowner Hávarður were very restless in the summer and early one morning a shepherd came home and Ólafur asked how it went.

"It is going so," he says, "that plenty of sheep are missing. I can not both look for those that are missing and tend those which are found."

Ólafur answers: "Be cheerful, comrade. Keep those that are found and I shall look for those that are missing."

He then becomes the most promising man and the handsomest of men to look at, big and strong. He was then eighteen winters old.

He now takes an ax in his hand then walks out along the fjord all the way until he comes to Lónseyri. He sees where all the sheep have come where they had been moved. Ólafur turns then to the farm. It was early in the morning. He knocked on the door. Then Sigríður went to the door and welcomed Ólafur well.

He took her greeting well. And when they had chatted a while, then Sigríður said: "A boat is going there from beyond the fjord and I see clearly that Þorbjörn Þjódrekur's son is there and Vakur his kinsman. I see that their weapons lay in the forestem. There is also Warflame, Þorbjörn's sword, and either he has done ill or he intends to and I want, Ólafur, that you do not meet Þorbjörn. There has long been anger between you two but I think there is no improvement, as you assessed my wealth at Laugaból."

Ólafur answers: "I do not fear Þorbjörn while I have not done anything against him. Neither will I back off from him alone."

She answers: "That is boldly said that you, eighteen winters, will not look away from that man who is battle-equal to any man. He also has the sword which chops clean though anything. I also suppose that, if they want to meet you, which my mind tells me would be, that Vakur, the evil man, will not sit by if you fight."

Ólafur answers: "I have no errand with Þorbjörn. I will not seek them but if we meet each other you shall have something bold to ask about if it is necessary."

Sigríður answers and says she will not ask. Ólafur sprang up quickly and bid her to live well and she bid him fare well.

He then went down to the tongue where the sheep lay. Þorbjörn and Vakur had then come to land opposite there. He then walks down to the boat and hauled and pulled the boat under them up onto the tongue. Þorbjörn then welcomed Ólafur well. Ólafur took his greeting and asked, where he was going.

He says he intended to find his sister Þórdís "and we will all go together."

Ólafur answers: "That will not work because I must herd my sheep home. It would be truly said that the sheepherders in Ísafjörður are becoming greater, if you lower yourself so."

"I do not go along with that," says Þorbjörn.

There was a big wide wood pile on the tongue and on it lay a big fork and it was broken on the ends. Ólafur took up the

The Saga of Hávarður of Ísafjörður 55

fork and had it in his hand, now he drives the sheep in front of him. They all walk together. Þorbjörn talks with Ólafur and was the most cheerful. He found that they always wanted to hang back but he was aware of it and so all went evenly forward and all forward in front of the hill. There the paths separated.

Þorbjörn then turns and said: "Kinsman Vakur, no need to delay that which is planned."

Ólafur then sees what they plan. He turns up the slope, but they attacked from below. Ólafur defends himself with the fork but Þorbjörn chops hard and fast with the sword Warflame and so sliced the fork like a stalk. But they got great blows from the fork, while it lasted. And when it was sliced apart Ólafur took his ax and defended himself so well that it seemed to them uncertain how it would go with them. And they were all wounded.

Þórdís Þorbjörn's sister went out that morning when they fought and heard it but could not see. She sent her servant to inquire. He did so and told Þórdís that Þorbjörn her brother, Vakur her son, and Ólafur Hávarður's son fought. She then returns and found Skarfur her son and tells him this news and asked him to go and help his kinsmen.

He said: "I am determined to fight with Ólafur and against them. It seems to me also a shame that three would go at one man because it is not as hopeless for them as for four others. I will by no means go."

Þórdís answers: "I thought that I had two bold sons. It is true as is said that much is long hidden. Now I know, that you are a daughter rather than a son when you dare not defend your kinsmen. I shall now also prove that I am a manlier daughter than you are a son."

She then went away but he got vehemently angry and sprang up and seized his ax. He leapt out and down the bank to where they fought. Þorbjörn saw him and attacked eagerly but Ólafur did not see him. And when Skarfur came in chopping range to Ólafur then he chopped two handed between Ólafur's shoulders, so that the ax was buried. Ólafur had intended to chop at Þorbjörn. And when Ólafur got the chop, he turned. Skarfur had lost the ax and Ólafur had swung his ax and chopped Skarfur in the head so that it stood at once in the brain. And just then Þorbjörn had come up by them and chopped in Ólafur's chest. And that was a sufficient death wound and they both fall. Þorbjörn then went to Ólafur and chopped across the face so that the teeth and molars sprang out.

Vakur asked: "Why are you doing that to a dead man?"

He said it might come to something. Þorbjörn then took a cloth and knotted the teeth in it and kept them. After that they went up to the farm and told Þórdís the news. They were both very much wounded. She now became extremely distressed with this story and grieved that she had egged her son on so much. But she now still gave them hospitality and nursing.

Now this news spreads all over Ísafjörður, and everyone thought Ólafur was the greatest loss from the defense which people heard he had made. Þorbjörn also acted well in that he told what had happened and well supported Ólafur's story. They went home as soon as they could and weariness ran from them.

Þorbjörn came to Lónseyri and asked after Sigríður. It was told him that she had not been found after she went out with Ólafur that morning. She was widely looked for and it is said that she was never found again. Then Þorbjörn went home and stayed quietly in his house.

CHAPTER 5

There is now to take up the story that Hávarður and Bjargey hear this news, the fall of Ólafur, their son. Old man Hávarður sighed deeply and went to his bed. It was also so said that all the next twelve months he lay in bed and never rose out of it. But Bjargey took the decision that she would row to sea each day with Þórhallur and she worked at night

The Saga of Hávarður of Ísafjörður 57

as she needed. So now the seasons went on and all is quiet. No prosecution happens about Ólafur. It also seemed not likely to people that any redress would come to his kinsmen because Hávarður seemed to them capable of nothing, and with such mighty men who were also not very likely to be fair. And the seasons now passed.

It was one morning that Bjargey went to meet with old man Hávarður and asked him whether he was awake. And he said he was awake and asked what she wanted.

"I want," she says, "that you stand up and go to Laugaból and find Þorbjörn and ask him compensation for Ólafur your son. It is manly for the one who is capable of no hardiness to not spare the tongue to say that which might cause him gain. You must not be exacting, if he acts well."

He answers: "I do not think well about this but you shall decide it."

After that old man Hávarður dresses and walks until he comes to Laugaból. Þorbjörn welcomed him well. Hávarður took his greeting.

Then old man Hávarður said: "Matters are such Þorbjörn," he said, "that I have come to demand compensations for Ólafur my son whom you killed for no reason."

Þorbjörn answers: "It is known Hávarður that I have killed many men. Even though people have said without reason I have not paid compensation for any. But because you had a manly son and it falls so near you then I think it is better to remember you somewhat though it be little. There is a horse over there in the hay yard which the boys call Dött. He is gray in color, very old and sore-backed and he has lain on his back unable to rise until now. But he has now been at the waste hay some days and I think he has improved. You go home with the horse if you want and have it."

Hávarður reddened and could answer nothing. He immediately went away and was extremely angry and Vakur shouted at him. And he walked down to his boat and went all bent up, and Þórhallur had waited there meanwhile. Then they rowed home. Hávarður went at once to his bed and lay himself down and never stood up during the next twelve months.

This got around and it seemed Þorbjörn had again shown unfairness and wickedness with this response. Now the seasons pass.

CHAPTER 6

And in the summer Þorbjörn rides to assembly with his men from Ísafjörður.

It is then one day again that Bjargey goes to talk with Hávarður. Then he asked what she wanted.

She answers: "Now I intend that you should ride to assembly and see if anything changes about your case."

He answers: "That is much against my disposition. Or does it seem to you that I have not been a little abused by Þorbjörn from my son's death, even though he not abuse me more there where all the aristocrats come together?"

"It will not go so," she says. "I guess that now there will be some helpers in your case and Gestir Oddleifur's son will do it. And if it goes as I guess, that he comes to a settlement with you and Þorbjörn and is assigned to pay you much wealth, then I guess that he will have many men by and a ring will surround you and there will be few of you inside the ring there where Þorbjörn pays the wealth. And if it so happens before the wealth is paid that Þorbjörn does something which is against your disposition or tries to, then you shall speed away as best as you can. And if you become then more active than you would expect then you shall not settle on this case because there is hope, though it be unlikely, that there would be vengeance for Ólafur our son. But if you are not more active then then you should not go unreconciled from the assembly because then there will be no vengeance."

He said he did not know what this would lead to—"and if I knew that there would be vengeance for Ólafur my son then I would never care, what I endure thereto."

CHAPTER 7

After that she prepares for his journey and he rides on his way. He was a rather bent old man and he comes to assembly. Then booths were tented and all the people had arrived. He rode to one great booth and it was the booth Steinþór of Eyrr had, a powerful man and great aristocrat and the most warlike and gallant. He dismounts and goes in to the booth. There sat Steinþór and his men by him. Hávarður went in front of him and greeted him well. Steinþór took his greeting well and asked who he was. Hávarður told of himself.

Steinþór said: "Are you the one who had the famous son, he who Þorbjörn killed and people praised greatly his defense?

He said that he is the same,—"And I want landowner that you would let me be in your booth during the assembly."

He answers: "I certainly promise that. And be silent and little meddling. The boys are always pranksters, but there is much grief on your mind. You are badly off, old and capable of nothing."

It is said that old man Hávarður takes himself space some place in the booth, lays himself down there and never goes from his space. He never comes to his case with any person and much of the assembly passes.

It was one morning that Steinþór goes to Hávarður and said: "Why did you come here as you lay there like a client commoner* or an invalid?"

Hávarður answers: "I had intended to look for compensation for Ólafur my son but I am very unwilling to. Þorbjörn is

---

*Steinþór refers to Hávarður as an "*árftökukarl* ." We use the term "client commoner" to convey the sense of dependency suggested by the first part of the term, which indicates a person who gives his wealth to a chieftain in return for support, as well as the commoner status indicated by the second part. Here the term implies helplessness.

unsparing in abuse and dishonor."

Steinþór said: "Take my advice, go to a meeting with Þorbjörn and plead your case. I expect if Gestir goes with you that you will get right of Þorbjörn."

Then he stood up and went out very bent. He went to the booth of Gestir and Þorbjörn and went into the booth. Þorbjörn was there but not Gestir. Þorbjörn greeted Hávarður and asked what he had come there for.

He answers: "The killing of Ólafur my son is so memorable to me, that it seems to me as newly done and it is my errand to ask you compensation for the killing."

Þorbjörn answers: "Here I know good advice. Come to me at home in the district. I will then comfort you somewhat but I have much to take care of now and I want that you not grumble to me now."

He answers: "If you do not allow for it now, then I have tried at home in your district where you do not either. I had intended, that someone would strengthen my case."

Þorbjörn spoke: "Hear a strange thing," he says. "He intends to make people come against me. Be away and do not come to me with this case again if you want to be unmaimed."

Then Hávarður got very angry and turns out from the booth and said: "We have become old and my days have been when it had seemed unlikely to me that I would tolerate such unfairness."

And when he goes away then people walk towards him. It was Gestir Oddleifur's son and his followers. Hávarður was so angry that he hardly thought about where he went. And he does not want to meet the men. He walked home to the booth. Gestir looked at the man who walked by him.

Hávarður went to his space and lay himself down and sighed deeply. Steinþór asked how it had gone. He told how it went.

Steinþór answers: "Such unfairness is unheard of and great shame is likely near where it comes from."

And when Gestir came in to the booth Þorbjörn greeted him well.

Gestir then said: "What man went from the booth a little while ago?"

Þorbjörn answers: "Why do you ask so extraordinarily, wise man? Many more go in and out here than we may distinguish."

Gestir answers: "This man was unlike other people. He was very large and somewhat of age and stumbling on his feet although the most manly and so it appeared to me he was filled up with grief and misery and provocation and he was so angry that he did not notice where he went. It appeared to me also that the man was lucky and it would not turn out well for most to have to do with him."

Þorbjörn answers: "It must have been old man Hávarður my assembly-man."

Gestir asked: "Was it not his son, who you killed for no reason?"

"I certainly think so," says he.

Gestir spoke: "How well do you think that you have fulfilled that which you promised me when I married my sister to you?"

A man was called Þorgils and he was named after his mother and called Halla's son. He was a most excellent man and gallant. He was then with Gestir his kinsman and at this time he was at his peak. Gestir asked Þorgils to go after Hávarður and invite him to come there. Þorgils went to Hávarður's booth and told him that Gestir wanted to meet him.

Hávarður answered: "I am unwilling to go and have to tolerate Þorbjörn's unfairness and shameful words."

Þorgils asked him to go, "Gestir will support your case."

Hávarður went even though he is unwilling to. They come to Gestir. Gestir stands up opposite him and welcomed him, Gestir seats him by his side.

Then Gestir said: "Now, Hávarður, you will take it up at the beginning and tell of your exchanges with Þorbjörn."

Now he did so. And when he had told, Gestir asked Þorbjörn whether any of it were so. Þorbjörn said he did not falsify.

Gestir said: "Has anyone heard such unfairness?" There are two choices here. The one, that I cancel all our agreements, else let me alone decide and settle your case."

Þorbjörn agrees to it.

Then they went out of the booth. Gestir called many people to him and people stood in a ring. And in the ring some people had come together and talked about the case.

Then said Gestir: "Þorbjörn, I cannot make it as much as it should be because you do not have it. I will make for Ólafur's killing a triple man-payment. And for the other unfairness which you have done to Hávarður I want to offer to you, Hávarður, fall and spring, that you come to me and I will honor you with gifts and promise you to never treat you like a common worker while we both live."

Then Þorbjörn said: "I will agree to this and will pay readily at home in my district."

Gestir answered: "Now you shall pay all the wealth here at the assembly and pay well and boldly, I will put in one man-payment."

He at once had it put forward all well paid. Hávarður then sat down and collected it in his cape. Þorbjörn also paid little by little and got payment of one man-payment and then said that ended what he had. Gestir asked him not to delay.

Þorbjörn then takes a knotted cloth and loosens it. "I will be certain that it will not seem to him underpaid if this goes with it," then he strikes Hávarður's nose so that blood fell at once on him. "There are now teeth and molars," says Þorbjörn, "from Ólafur your son."

Hávarður now sees that the teeth tumble down on to his cape. He springs up furious so that each coin bounces its own way. He had a staff in his hand and leaps at the ring and the staff jabs at the chest of one man who falls over backwards at once, so that he long lay witless. Hávarður vaulted out over the ring of men so that he came in contact with none and came down far away and so home to the booth like a young man. And when he came home he would speak with no one and threw himself down and lay as if he were sick.

After this Gestir said to Þorbjörn: "You are like no person for evil and unfairness. And I do not know how to see into a man if you or your kinsmen do not regret this some time."

Gestir was then so angry and furious that he rides at once from the assembly to Ísafjörður and makes a divorce between Þorbjörn and Þorgerður. Now it seems to Þorbjörn and all his kinsmen, that this was the greatest loss, but they can do nothing. Gestir said that he would suffer other losses and greater ones and they would be more fitting. Gestir rides to Barðaströnd with his kinswoman and wealth.

So it is said that after the assembly old man Hávarður prepares to go home. He was then all stiff.

Then Steinþór said: " Hávarður if you need a little support then come to me."

Hávarður thanked him, then rode home and lay down in his bed and lay there the third twelve months. He was then the very stiffest. Bjargey held on the same with her work, that she rowed to sea each day with Þórhallur.

CHAPTER 8

It was one day in the summer when they were at sea that they saw a boat going out of the fjord; they also recognized that it was Þorbjörn and his homemen.

Then Bjargey said: "Now we shall take up our lines and row toward Þorbjörn. I want to meet him. You shall row in front of the stem of the boat and I shall talk with Þorbjörn a bit and you shall row around the boat in the meantime."

They now do that, row to the boat.

Bjargey now casts a word at Þorbjörn. She greets him and asks where he intends to go. He says he shall go west to Vaðill,—"There Sturla my brother and Þjóðrekur his son have come out. I shall move them here to me."

She asked: "How long will you be away, landowner?" she says.

"Nearly a week," he says.

Þórhallur had then rowed all around the boat. Bjargey had some bag in her hand and waved it all around the boat. And when she has done such as she wanted they lift the oars and row away with all their strength.

Then Þorbjörn said: "There goes the most wretched of a women, and we shall at once row after them and kill him and maim her."

Then Brandur said: "Now you again prove that which is said of you, that you will not hold back from the worst, and I will help Bjargey and Þórhallur as I can; then you will get what you bargain for."

With Brandur's conversation and because they had got far away, Þorbjörn let it be and went on his way.

Then said Bjargey: "It is not likely but it is my thought that there will be vengeance for Ólafur my son. We will not go home."

"Where do you want to go, then?" says Þórhallur.

"Now we shall go," she says, " and meet Valbrandur my brother."

He lived at Valbrandsstaðir. He was a very old man but had been the most excellent man. He had two sons, the most promising men. One was called Torfi and the other Eyjólfur. They were then young in age.

They did not rest until they came there. Valbrandur was out in the hayfield and many men with him. He then went to meet his sister and welcomed her well and asked her to stay there. But she said it would not suit her, "I must return this evening."

He asked, "What do you want then, sister?"

"I want you to lend me your seal nets."

He answered, "Here are three nets and one is very old and now not trustworthy, but has been reliable but two are new and untried. You can have what you want, two or three."

She answers: "I want to have the new ones as I do not want to risk taking the old one. But have them prepared when I have them sent for."

He said it would be so.

After that they went away.

Then Þórhallur said: "Where shall we go now?"

She answers: "Now we shall go and meet Þorbrandur my brother."

He lived at Þorbrandsstaðir. He was then very old. He had two young sons. One was called Oddur and the other Þórir. They were promising men.

And when they came there Þorbrandur welcomed them well and asked them to stay there. She said they can not.

"What do you want then sister," he says.

"I want," she says, "you to lend me your nets."

He answers: "I have three, and one is very old but two are new and have not been used. Have whichever you want two or three." She said she would have the new, and with that they separated.

Then they went away.

Þórhallur asked: "Where shall we go now?"

"Now we shall," she says, "go to meet old man Ásbrandur, my brother."

He lived at Ásbrandsstaðir. He was the eldest of the brothers. He was married to the sister of old man Hávarður. He had a son who was called Hallgrímur. He was young in age but both big and strong, unhandsome looking, although manly.

And when Bjargey comes there Ásbrandur welcomes her well and asked her to stay there. She said she would go home in the evening.

He asked: "What do you want then and you come so seldom to meet your kinsman?"

"The errand is little," she says. "We are so unprovided with turf tools and I would be glad if you lend me your turf ax."

He answers smiling: "Here are two and one is a very rusty weapon, old and notched, and now thought fit for nothing. The other is new and big and has been used for nothing."

And she said she wants to have the new one, "when I have it fetched."

He answers that she shall decide.

Then they go home to Hávarðsstaðir in the evening.

CHAPTER 9

Now some days pass until it seemed to her likely that Þorbjörn would come from the west. And one day she went to Hávarður's bed and asked, whether he slept.

He sat up and said a verse:

Verse 2

Sleep has not come to my eyes since,
-he, the worthy viking,
died from me for a swords edge,
-since, the killing men attacked
swiftly with roaring of the sword,
they who fell Ólafur for no reason.

"It is certain," she says, "That this is a very great lie, that you have never slept in three years. But now it is time to stand up and behave yourself manfully if you want to avenge Ólafur your son because he will not be avenged in your life, if not on this night."

And when he heard her words, he sprang up out of the bed and onto the floor and then said a verse.

Verse 3

In my old age I don't have to tell any more about my feat.
People, grant me silence willingly
Since I knew the manly warrior
after he was killed,
My famous son, my pillar and support is
certainly killed.

Hávarður was then the most spirited and did not walk with a limp. He went to a large chest, it was full of weapons, and

The Saga of Hávarður of Ísafjörður

opened it, put a helmet on his head and put on a strong mail coat. He then looked up and saw that a seagull flew by the window. He then spoke a verse:

Verse 4

The raven is eager as he approaches a pool of blood.
Tired from his flying,
he demands a morning kill.
So cried the battle raven
when the warriors were death bound
(as Odin's ravens foretold).

He armed himself quickly and deftly. He also prepared Þórhallur with good weapons. And when they were prepared he turned to Bjargey and kissed her, then said it was not clear when they would next meet.

She bid him fare well. "I do not need to have egging on words with you about revenge for Ólafur our son because I know, there follow eagerness and prowess where you are."

After that they separated. Hávarður and Þórhallur went down to the sea, pushed out a six oared boat and take to the oars, did not let up until they came to Valbrandur's farm. There was a long spit of land which went out in the sea. They laid the boat there. Hávarður asked Þórhallur to watch the boat and he went up to the farm. He had a spear in hand. It was an excellent weapon. And when he came up to the field, they, father-and-sons, were there. The brothers were undressed and raked up hay. They had taken off their shoes and set them on the ground by them. They were high top shoes. Valbrandur went toward Hávarður and welcomed him well and asked him to stay there.

He said he could not stay there: "I have come to fetch your seal nets which you lent your sister."

Valbrandur went to his sons and said: "Your in-law Hávarður has come here, and is dressed as if he would intend some great deed."

And when they hear that they throw the rakes down and run to their clothes. And when they were to put on their shoes, they had stiffened in the sun. They pulled them on quickly, so that the skin went at once from their heels. And when they came home the shoes were full of blood.

Valbrandur got his sons good weapons and said: "Give Hávarður good backing. Think more on revenge than what is coming after."

After that they went to Þorbrandsstaðir. Oddur and Þórir were also quickly prepared. Now they went until they came to Ásbrandsstaðir. There Hávarður claimed the turf ax. Then his kinsman Hallgrímur prepared himself for the journey with Hávarður.

A man is named Ánn. He was a homeman of Ásbrandur. He had houseservant's work. He was Hallgrímur's foster father and prepared himself for the journey with them. And when they were prepared they go to where the boat was. Þórhallur welcomed them well. They were then eight together and each more warlike than the other.

Then Hallgrímur said to his kinsman Hávarður: "Why did you go so from home, kinsman, that you had neither sword nor ax." He answers: "If it so happens that we find Þorbjörn Þjóðrekur's son after we separate you shall say otherwise because I intend to get the sword Warflame which is the best of weapons."

They said to him well said, "Now for us much would depend on taking ourselves in hand manfully."

It was very late in the day. They then pushed off the boat and boarded and took to the oars. They saw that a great flock of ravens flew in front of them and over the spit of land ahead of them.

Hávarður then said a verse:

Verse 5

> I must bring the raven meat as I promised.
> The hungry raven flies over the spit.
> I know, Hallgrímur
> that we will have a lucky journey.
> That is well.
> I hear the sound of clashing swords in my ears.

They went across the sound and it was blowing very hard in the fjord and they took in much water. They sat firm and did not let up until they came to Laugaból. It was good to lay in because Þorbjörn had had made a good harbor there. He had had it cleared and cleaned the shore. There was a great depth. A boat could float there or a bigger ship if one wanted. There were also big ribs buried for boat-rollers and fastened on the ends with rocks, there no man need get wet when stepping from a ship or onto a ship whether it was a larger or smaller ship. And up above was a high pebble ridge. Above the ridge stood a great doored boatshed and it was well looked after. On one side there was a big inlet above the ridge. From the boatshed one saw nothing on the beach but from the pebble ridge one could see both to the boatshed and to the beach. And when they come to land they leap from the boat.

Then Hávarður said: "Now we shall carry the boat up over the ridge to the inlet. We shall also be above the ridge so that they may not see us at once. Let us also not be too eager; let no one jump up before I say to."

It was then very dark.

CHAPTER 10

There is now to take up the story that Þorbjörn and his companions went from the west ten together in the boat. Sturla was there and Þjóðrekur his son, Þorbjörn and Vakur, Brandur the strong and two houseservants. Their boat was heavily laden. And that same evening they come to Laugaból before dark.

Then Þorbjörn said: "We shall not go hastily and we shall let the boat lie here tonight and not carry anything from it except our weapons and clothes. The weather now is good and dry. Vakur, you shall carry up our weapons."

He took first their swords and spears and carried them up to the boatshed.

Then Torfi said: "Let us take first their swords and the one comes with them."

"Let us wait," said Hávarður.

He asked Hallgrímur to go and take the sword Warflame and bring it to him. And when Vakur went down Hallgrímur leapt and took the sword and brought it to Hávarður. He raised it aloft and shook the hilt.

Vakur went up the second time and had piled the shields on his back and had piled steel caps on his arms. He wore a helmet on his head. And when he had come up to the inlet they leapt up and intended to take him. And when he hears their clatter it seemed to him that there would be hostilities. He wanted to hurry to Þorbjörn and his men with the weapons. But when he turns hard around his feet slipped by the inlet so that his head comes down first under him. It was very wet but the water shallow and the man was weighted down with all the weapons. But he can not stand up. No one would help him and so ends Vakur's life that he dies there.

And when they saw that they leap up to the pebble ridge. And when Þorbjörn sees this he throws himself at once in the sound and swims from land. Old man Hávarður is the first to see it, he speeds at once and throws himself into the sound after Þorbjörn.

So it is said of Brandur the strong that he leaps to and tears up one boat-roller that was a large whale rib and whacks Hallgrímur's foster father in the head. Hallgrímur had then come down from the ridge and saw that Ánn fell. He leapt with his ax ready and chopped Brandur in the head and cleaved him down to the shoulders. And at that moment

The Saga of Hávarður of Ísafjörður 71

Þorbjörn and Hávarður leapt into the sound. And when he sees that, he leaps at once after them. Torfi Valbrandur's son leaps toward Sturla. He was both big and strong and no man in better fighting shape. He also had all his weapons. They fought both long and manfully.

CHAPTER 11

Now it must be taken up where Þorbjörn and Hávarður are. They swim from land. It was a long swim until Þorbjörn came to a line of rocks which lies off there. And when Þorbjörn comes to the rocks Hávarður approached head on. And when Þorbjörn sees that he was weaponless he grabs up a big stone and intended to drive it into his head. And when Hávarður sees that, it came into his mind that he had heard it said from outside the land that there was another custom announced than in the northern lands and, with it, if someone could tell him that the belief were better and more beautiful then he would believe it if he could overcome Þorbjörn. And after that he swam as fast as he could to the rocks. And when Þorbjörn was about to throw the rock his feet slipped and it was slippery on the stones so that he fell backwards and the stone falls down on his chest and he becomes stunned. And just then Hávarður comes up on the rocks and at once ran him through with the sword Warflame. Hallgrímur had then come up on the rocks. Hávarður hacked then across Þorbjörn's face and cleaved the teeth and molars and down across the face. Hallgrímur asked, why he did so with a dead man. Hávarður answered: "It was in my mind then when Þorbjörn shoved the knotted cloth in my face. Out of it fell teeth and molars which he had chopped out of Ólafur my son with the same sword."

Then they swam to land. It seemed to people then, those who told about it, Hallgrímur had behaved valiantly when he swam out in the fjord and did not know that there was a rock out there. It was a very long swim though.

And when they came to land it was all calm. And when they came up on the ridge a man leapt at them with a ready ax. He had on a blue shirt and belted in his britches. They turn toward him and when they met they recognized there Torfi Valbrandur's son and they welcomed him well. Torfi asked whether Þorbjörn was dead.

Hávarður said a verse:

Verse 6

> I cleaved the warrior all down through the jaw;
> I let one chop come in his eyes;
> I didn't see it, the sword with
> ornamented guard give way;
> Warflame rode to the blow,
> and I saw him, mighty warrior, fall.

Hávarður asked what they had done. Torfi said, that Sturla had fallen and the houseservants,—"but Ánn is dead."

Hávarður said a verse:

Verse 7

> We have now felled four of them,
> who let Bjargey's son die in his own blood.
> I count our gain in it.
> Hallgrímur says now one is fallen of our men.
> The battle was fierce.
> The houseservant was knocked dead
> with a boat-roller.

Then they went up to the boatshed. Their companions were there and welcomed them well. Then Eyjólfur Valbrandur's son asked whether they should not kill the slaves.

Hávarður said Ólafur his son would not be more revenged if they killed the slaves. "Let them stay here tonight and

The Saga of Hávarður of Ísafjörður

watch so that no one steals from the wreckage."

Then Hallgrímur asks what they should do then.

Hávarður answers: "We shall take the boat and all that seems to us worth it and head to Mánaberg and meet Ljótur the champion. There would be more revenge in such a man as he is if things would turn out that well."

They now take the boat and many possessions which the kinsmen had had and row out along the fjord and to Mánaberg.

Then Hávarður said: "Now we must go with a plan. Ljótur is wary for himself. He always has many enemies. He has himself watched over every night with weapons. He lies in a locked bed closet every night. In the bed closet is a tunnel and one tunnel mouth is behind the house. He also has many men with him."

Then Torfi Valbrandur's son said: "It is my advice that we bring fire to the farm and burn every man's child inside."

Hávarður said that such shall not be: "You and kinsman Hallgrímur shall be up on the house and take care of the tunnel mouth which he may go out. I trust you both best for that. Here are also two doors in front of the house. In the hall are also two doors. Now shall Eyjólfur and I go in one and the brothers Oddur and Þórir the other and so into the hall and you, Þórhallur, shall take care of the boat here and you shall defend it manfully if it is necessary."

And when he has arranged so as he wants then they go to the farmhouse. A big out-building stood in the field and a man sat under the wall with weapons. And when they come nearly up to him he sees the men and springs up and leaps and intends to give warning of their coming. Hallgrímur went first of the companions. He flung a spear after him and it ran him through near the wall. He died at once on the spear. After that they went there where they had planned. Torfi and Hallgrímur go to where there was an exit from the house.

CHAPTER 12

It is said that Hávarður springs quickly into the hall. A light burned there and it was light above but dark below. He went there at once to the bed closet. It so happened that the housewife had not then come to bed, she was in the hall and women with her. The bedcloset was not locked. Hávarður strikes the flat of the sword on the door. Ljótur woke with that and asked who clattered. Old man Hávarður said his name.

Then Ljótur said: "Why are you here, old man Hávarður? We were told day before yesterday that you were nearly dead."

Hávarður answers: "You should sooner ask about another's death. I know to tell you of the killing of your brothers, Þorbjörn and Sturla."

And when he hears that he leaps up in the bed and grabs down a sword which hung above him. Ljótur asked people to stand up in the hall and take to weapons. Then Hávarður leapt up in the bed closet and chopped at Ljótur on the left shoulder but Ljótur turned hard and the sword slipped off the shoulder and sliced down his arm and sliced the hand off at the elbow joint. Ljótur leapt out of the bed with his drawn sword and intended to chop at Hávarður. Then Eyjólfur had come up and chopped at the right shoulder and chopped off the hand and they felled Ljótur there. Then was a great bustle in the hall. Ljótur's houseservants then wanted to stand up and take to weapons. Þorbrandur's sons had then come in. People then got a few blows and scratches.

Hávarður then spoke and asked the houseservants to be as still as possible, to show no hint of ill, "else we will kill every man's child one after the other."

It seemed to them best to lie as still as possible. Ljótur was lamented by few although they had been with him. After that Hávarður and his men leave. Hávarður did not want to do more there. Then Torfi and Hallgrímur came towards them.

The Saga of Hávarður of Ísafjörður

They had meant to join in and they asked what had happened.

Hávarður then said a verse:

Verse 8

Eyjólfur was quick when he
fought that powerful man.
I heard that he hastily drew a sharp sword
Eyjólfur, the champion, still remembers other battle with
  the men
and to give to killers a fair return.

Then they went down to the boat and Þórhallur greeted them well. Then Torfi Valbrandur's son asked what they should do now.

"Now we shall look for some support. Although there has not been as much revenge as I want we will not alone suffice to carry though this work. There are still many kinsmen of Þorbjörn, they who are of much esteem. It seems to me likeliest to look to Steinþór of Eyrr. He more than others offered me support if I needed any."

They all asked him to see to it and said they wanted to do as he wanted and not to separate until he thought it advisable. After that they set out in the fjord. They took a grip on the oars and Hávarður sat at the helm. Then Hallgrímur spoke and asked Hávarður to say a verse.

Then Hávarður said this verse:

Verse 9

We had all together, Hallgrímur,
paid Þjóðrekur's sons for
their very devilish spite;
I regretted not this killing;
Hostile men were killed for the fault of their worth;
I know that the revenge called after
Þorbjörn must come to me.

CHAPTER 13

Now there is nothing to tell of their trip until they came to Eyrr. It was at that time of day when Steinþór sat at table with his men. They go into the hall four together with their weapons. Hávarður went in front of Steinþór and greeted him. Steinþór took his greeting and asked who he was. He said he was called Hávarður.

"Were you in our booth last summer?"

He said it was so.

Steinþór said: "Boys, have you seen a man now more unlike himself then? It appeared to me as if he could hardly go staffless between booths, and he seemed to us likely to be a bedridden man because he was very vexed. But now the man appears to me the most accomplished with weapons. And is there some news to tell?"

Hávarður answered: "We tell of the killing of Þorbjörn Þjóðrekur's son and his brothers, Ljótur and Sturla Þjóðrekur's sons, Brandur the strong, altogether seven."

Steinþór answers: "That is big news. And who have done this who have cut down the greatest champions and mighty men?"

Hávarður spoke and said that he and his kinsmen had done it. Steinþór spoke and asked where Hávarður intended to look for protection after such great work. Hávarður answers:

"I had planned as now I have done to look to you. It seemed to me you said it last summer at assembly that I might come to you no less than to other aristocrats."

Steinþór answers: "I do not know when you think yourself to need great support if now you need little. But you may think that I would not receive you well when you were in need if I am late to grant it now. It shall not be so. I want to invite you, Hávarður, to stay here with your companions while this matter is going on. I will also to promise to redress your cases after this one because it seems to me you are such a man that one would be better off who supports you and it is not

The Saga of Hávarður of Ísafjörður

certain that they would get as vigorous men as you are. This has gone more according to circumstance than likelihood."

Hávarður then said a verse:

Verse 10

Now is the occasion for men
who want to support us to step forward.
Men say that the pride of Ísafjörður
is unprotected
and is still being attacked
and damaged by the sword of faultless men.

They thanked Steinþór for his generous invitation. He asked to take their clothing and weapons and get them dry clothes. And when Hávarður took his helmet off and drops his mail-coat, then he said a verse:

Verse 11

The enemies laughed and
made fun at my expense.
The death of my son falls on their heads.
Let them pay for death of my son differently
in every cliff by the sea,
since the widely known villains
were killed with swords.

Steinþór asked Hávarður to go to the benches and sit across from him,—"and place your companions there by you."

Hávarður does so, places Hallgrímur his kinsman next to him on the seat away from the door, by Hallgrímur's side sit Þórir and Oddur Þorbrandur's sons and on Hávarður's side, toward the door sat Torfi and Eyjólfur Valbrandur's sons, then Þórhallur, then the homemen who had been sitting there.

And when they sat down, then Hávarður said a verse:

Verse 12

Hallgrímur, we shall await
the cowards calmly at home.
I settled for telling it as it is.
I expect the worst;
But none of the killings
which we have made will ever be compensated for.
I will never pay weath for compensation with these men.

Then Steinþór said: "It is now evident Hávarður that most things are going as you want. And it would also be so if there were no prosecution from men as strong and powerful as all the kinsmen and as great men as there are still for the prosecution.

Hávarður says of himself that he never thinks about the prosecution: from here on it was closed, he would have no sorrow or anger in his heart, and would think that his case would not end any other way than well. He was so cheerful and happy with every man's child as if he were young.

This news spread widely and seemed to most to be unlikely.

They stayed now at Eyrr with landowner Steinþór. They did not lack a large crowd or joy. There were no fewer than sixty fighting men.

Let us now turn from them where they stay at Eyrr with Steinþór at great cost and in greatest joy.

CHAPTER 14

A man was called Ljótur. He lived at Rauðasandur. He was called Dueling-Ljótur. He was both big and strong and the greatest dueler. He was a brother of Þorbjörn Þjóðrekur's son. It is so said, that Ljótur was the most unfair man and had an ax in the head of any person who did not give him what he

The Saga of Hávarður of Ísafjörður

wanted and no one walked carefree there in Rauðasandur and many other places.

A man was called Þorbjörn. He lived at the place called Eyrr. He was a man rich in wealth and well up in age and not a great man in disposition. He had two sons. One was called Grímur and the other Þorsteinn.

So it is said that Ljótur and Þorbjörn had one irrigated meadow together. It was the greatest treasure. It was so divided that each should have it in alternative summers. And below Ljótur's farm was a creek which flooded the meadow in spring. There were dams in the creek and it was well arranged. It always went so that when Þorbjörn was to have the meadow that he never got the creek and so it happened that Ljótur next put out the word that Þorbjörn did not have a share in it and he should not dare to claim it. And when Þorbjörn heard that it seems to him that Ljótur will do what he has promised. There was a short distance between their farms.

And one day they met. Þorbjörn asked whether Ljótur intended to take the meadow from him.

Ljótur answered and told him not to say anything more about this, "It will not help you more than anyone else to complain about what I want to keep. Either let yourself well like what I want to do or else I will drive you off your property. You shall have neither the meadow nor anything else."

And when Þorbjörn knew Ljótur's unfairness, since he had excess wealth, he buys the meadow for what Ljótur said and gave twenty hundreds* at once for it and they separate with that.

---

*When Christianity came, Icelanders adopted the decimal hundred, as is used today, in ecclesiastical and scholastic matters, such as chronology, but in civil matters, law, exchange, and trade they used the older base twelve or duodecimal hundred—ten twelves, or ten dozens. Here, a "hundred" would be 120 rather than 100. A "hundred" referred to 120 ells (1 ell = 18 inches) of homespun wool or *vaðmal*. This was used as a unit of value for computing compensation, trade, and other transactions (Gelsinger 1981).

And when the boys heard of it they take it very badly and call it the greatest robbery to buy that which he had before. News of this now spread widely. It seemed to people the most unfair happening.

The brothers watched their father's sheep. Þorsteinn was twelve winters and Grímur ten.

It was one day in the beginning of winter when the brothers went to the sheep house, a strong wind had come, and they intended to find out whether all the livestock had come home. At the same time Ljótur had gone that morning to his driftage. He was a very active around his farm. It was at that time when the boys had come to the house that they see that Ljótur walks up from the shore.

Then said Þorsteinn to his brother Grímur: "Do you see Dueling-Ljótur there where he walks up from the sea?"

"How can I not see him?" says Grímur.

Then Þorsteinn said: "This Ljótur does great unfairness to us and many others and I am in a mood to avenge if I could."

Grímur said: "That is unwisely said that you would show some hostility from you to such a champion as Ljótur who is also worth more than four or five others though they be quite grown and he is not in a child's reach."

Þorsteinn answers: "It will not do to hold me back, I will do it anyway, but you will resemble your father and want to be a victim of Ljótur's robbery like many others."

Grímur says: "Because you have this in mind kinsman I will be of little use to you but such as it is I shall give to you according to my strength."

"Then you do well," says Þorsteinn, "and it may be, that it will go justly." They had handaxes in hand and they were little and biting-sharp. Now they stand and wait for Ljótur to come to the house. He turned quickly by them. Ljótur had a poleaxe in hand. He walks on his way and acts as if he does not see the boys. And when he passes by them Þorsteinn chops Ljótur's shoulder. The ax did not bite. But it was chopped so hard that the arm went out of the shoulder joint. And when Ljótur saw that the boys wanted to provoke him he turns quickly and heaves up the ax and intended to strike Þorsteinn with the ax. And just when he turns up the ax Grímur leaps and chops off Ljótur's hand from above the wrist. The hand with the ax then falls down. Then they left small space between chops and there is nothing more likely to be told but that they felled Dueling-Ljótur there and are not wounded. They bury him in the snow and go from there.

And when they come home their father was in the doorway and asked why they had been so late and why their clothes were bloody. They told of Ljótur's killing. He asks whether they had killed him. They say that it was so.

Then he said: "Be away, bad evil men; you have done the greatest misdeed and killed the greatest aristocrat and our leader. You will have caused this, that I will be done out of my belongings and all of that which I have and you will be killed and that is very well."

Þorbjörn then ran away out from the house.

Grímur said: "Let us have nothing to do with this monster who behaves so loathsomely and it is no average wretch who behaves so."

Þorsteinn answers: "Let us meet him because I suspect that he is not as angry as he acts."

After that they go to him. Þorbjörn spoke gladly with them and asked them to wait there. He then went home and was away a little while. He came back with two well prepared horses.

Then Þorbjörn said that they should mount: "I want to send you both to Eyrr to my friend Steinþór. Ask him to take you in. Here is a gold ring, a great treasure, which you shall give him. He has often asked for it and never got it but now I shall give it for both your needs."

After that the old man kissed his sons and told them fare well and that they will meet again in good health.

Now nothing is said of their trip until they come to Eyrr. It was early in the day. They go to the hall, and it was all hung with tapestry and benches on both sides were filled. There lacked neither noise nor gladness. They go in front of Steinþór and greet him well. He took their greeting well. He asked who they were. They said their names and their father's.

Then Þorsteinn said: "Here is a ring which my father sent to you and his greetings with it and asked that you give us winter quarters this winter or longer if we need it."

Steinþór took the ring and said: "Do you tell any news?" They tell then of the killing of Ljótur and that they had killed him.

Steinþór answers: "Again surprising things have happened, that two young men have done damage to such a champion as Ljótur was. And what was the reason?"

They told as it seemed to them.

Steinþór said: "It is my advice that you go over in front of Hávarður, the gray haired old man who sits across from me. Ask him whether he will take you into his company or not."

They now do so, go in front of Hávarður. He welcomes them well and asked the news and acts as if he had not heard and they told him in the greatest detail.

And when they had ended their speech Hávarður sprang up towards them and said a verse.

Verse 13

   I liked you from this kill.
   Be loyal to us warrior.
   I wish you champions still even longer life
   be my greatest joy.
   I hear the man (Ljótur) has been killed
   Let the people in the west hear more
   about what harms our enemies.

Hávarður seats the brothers at his side, toward the door. They sat there glad and cheerful.

Now this news was spread all over Rauðasandur and to many other places. Ljótur is found dead there under the wall. People then went to Þorbjörn and asked him. Þorbjörn did not deny that his sons had killed him. And as Ljótur was unpopular in Rauðasandur and Þorbjörn said he had responded angrily and driven his sons away, which his homemen agreed with, then there is no prosecution at that time. Þorbjörn sits calmly in his house.

CHAPTER 15

Now it is to take up that they sit at Eyrr all together doing well. It became expensive for Steinþór so great a crowd as he had and he needed to lay out great wealth for the generosity he maintained.

A man who lived at Otradalur was called Atli and had the sister of Steinþór of Eyrr, who was called Þórdís. Atli was the least of men and the most wretched-looking, and so it is said, that it would be according to his disposition that he was the greatest wretch, although he was from greater people and so rich that he hardly knew the count of his money. Þórdís had been married to Atli for wealth. So it is said that the farm at Otradalur is much out of the public way. It was out on the other side of the fjord across from Eyrr. Atli was too stingy to keep workmen. He worked both night and day such as he could. He was also so stubborn that he would have nothing with other people neither for good nor ill. He was the greatest farmer. He had a great outbuilding. In it were all kinds of good things. Inside were large piles and all kinds of meat, dried fish and cheese and all that was needed. Atli had made his bed there and they lay there every night.

So it is said that one morning Steinþór was afoot early and went to Hávarður's bed and took him by his feet and asked him to stand up. Hávarður sprang up quickly and onto to the floor. And when he stood up one after another of the companions stood up because it was their habit to all go wherever one needed to go. And when they were all dressed they went out in the house yard. Steinþór was there in front with some men.

Then Hávarður said: "We are prepared landowner, to go

wherever you want to have us go. We want to follow you eagerly whether it is favorable or unfavorable but it is according to my principle that I do not want to be on any journey, which I do not know where I shall go."

Steinþór answers: "I intend to go to my in-law Atli and I want you to give me help."

They went down to the sea. There was the boat which they had taken from Þorbjörn. They pushed the boat off and took to the oars and rowed across the fjord. It seemed to Steinþór that the companions take to everything hardily.

That morning landowner Atli stood up early and got out of his bed. Atli was so dressed that he was in a white shirt, short and tight. The man was not swift footed. He was both wretched and ugly to see, bald and hollow-eyed. He went out and looked at the weather. The weather was cold and very frosty. He saw that a boat went from across the fjord and was coming almost to land and recognized there landowner Steinþór his in-law and he was not pleased with this. There was a hay-yard in the farmyard and though more out in the field; near it stood a haystack and hay had been pulled off it from all sides. It was Atli's trick that he leapt into the yard and tumbled the haystack down on himself and Atli lay there under it.

Now it is to tell of Steinþór and all of them together that they come to land and go up to the farm. And when they come into the outbuilding then Þórdís sprang up and welcomed her brother well and all of them and said he was seldom seen there. Steinþór asks where his in-law Atli was. She said he had gone away a little while. Steinþór asked them to look for him. They looked for him around the farm and did not find him and then tell Steinþór.

Then Þórdís said: "What do you want of us here kinsman?"

He answered: "I had planned that Atli should have either given to me or sold to me some provisions."

She answered: "I think that I decide no less than Atli. I want you to have such as you want."

He said that he would very much want that. After that they

clear the storehouse and carry the goods down to the boat until it was loaded. There were all kinds of provisions.

Then Steinþór said: "Now you shall go home in the boat but I will stay here with my sister. I am curious to know how Atli my in-law will behave when he returns."

She answers: "I think that is useless my kinsman," said Þórdís. "It will not amuse you to hear him, but you will decide anyway. But you shall promise me not to be a worse friend to Atli than before whatever he says or does."

Steinþór agreed to this. She made him stay behind some hangings where no one could see him.

And they go home again in the boat. They had much sharp wind on the fjord and took much water inside, before they came to land.

CHAPTER 16

Now it is to take up when Atli lies under the haystack. And when he sees that they are away from land he creeps from under the haystack and he is then so stiff and frozen that he can hardly stand up, then he drags home to the storehouse. And when he comes in he shivers so much that each of his teeth jingles and rattles. He looks up and sees that the storehouse is cleared.

Then he said: "What robbers have come here?"

Þórdís answers: "No one has robbed here but Steinþór my brother came here with his men and I gave to him that which you call robbed."

Atli answered: "I will regret it most that I have got you and I am bereft of possessions. I do not know a person worse than Steinþór your brother or who are greater robbers than those who are with him and have now taken from me and stolen and robbed everything from here so that we will soon be begging house to house."

Then Þórdís said: "We will never lack for wealth and go into your bed and let me warm you a little. It seems to me you are very frozen."

And it happened that he crawls under the covers to her. It seems to Steinþór that his in-law looks far from mighty, with nothing on his feet and a shirt bunched up on his head that reached nowhere down below. Atli then slides under the covers to her and is speaking violently constantly blaming Steinþór and calling him a robber.

After that he is silent for a while.

And when he warms up then he said: "Although there is to say that I have a great treasure which you are, it is also true to say that one will not find such a generous man as my in-law Steinþór. It is also well what he has taken, it is as if I kept it."

This goes on for a long while that he praises Steinþór. Steinþór goes then in front of the bed and when Atli sees him he stands up and welcomes him.

Then Steinþór said: What go you think in-law Atli now that your storehouse is cleared?"

Atli answered: "It is most true that I think it best that you have them. I also want to invite you to have all of my goods that you want because there is no lack. You have taken up the most aristocratic way, taking in those men who have told their grief. You will want to send them home with generous gifts. You may become the greatest man from that."

Then Steinþór said: "I will ask you this in-law Atli that you not make yourself as wretched as you have made yourself before. Take yourself well up and have workmen for you and be sociable with other people. I know that you are not a small person though you make yourself so because of your disposition."

Atli now promised this. Steinþór went home that day, the in-laws separate with great friendliness, and Steinþór then came home to Eyrr and thinks this has gone well. They now sit home and the winter passes. They had much gladness at Eyrr during the winter. They played vigorous skin-ball games.

CHAPTER 17

A man was called Svartur. He was a slave there at Eyrr, big and strong, so that he had the power of four men. He was useful on the farm. He worked a lot.

It was one day that Steinþór had the slave called to him and said to him: "They want you to be in the game with us today because we lack one man."

Svartur answers: "There is no use asking me because I have much work to do. I also guess your champions do not want to work for me. Even though I shall grant you this if you want."

So it is told that Hallgrímur should be against Svartur. It is also best to tell that each time when they wrestled Svartur falls and after each fall his shoes come off and he is often delayed there tying his shoes. It goes on like that a large part of the day and people shouted and laughed a lot.

Hávarður said a verse:

Verse 14

The warriors Valbranður's sons,
from across the fjord
were not long tying their shoe laces
I recall this now-When I was to avenge the warrior, my
   son, this summer,
The stormy sea got wilder.

The game was the best. Hallgrímur was then eighteen winters old and seemed likely to be a valiant man when he was full-grown.

So it is said that the winter passed and there was nothing for news at all until they prepared for assembly. Steinþór pretended he did not know what he should arrange for those companions. He did not want to take them to assembly with him but it seemed not good to have them stay home during the assembly.

And a few days before the assembly he met Atli. Atli asked what he would arrange for the people staying with him during the assembly.

Steinþór said he did not know for certain where he should bring them so that he could be unafraid for them, "unless you take them."

Atli said: "I will bind myself to take these men."

"Then you do well," said Steinþór.

Atli said: "I will help them according to my power as you want."

Steinþór said: "I trust you well to do it."

CHAPTER 18

After that Hávarður and his companions went away with Atli. They came to Otradalur. He receives Hávarður with both hands. They lacked nothing which they needed. He made them the best feast. There were ten fighting men. Atli had the storehouse cleared and made their beds there and hung up their weapons and it was all prepared in the best way.

And Steinþór called on his men. There he lacked neither friends nor kinsmen. He was also related by marriage with aristocrats. He rode to assembly with three hundreds* of men. There were all his followers, friends, kinsmen, and in-laws.

CHAPTER 19

A man was called Þórarinn. He was a man with a chieftaincy west around Dýrafjörður, a great aristocrat and somewhat aged. He was the brother of Þjóðrekur's sons. He was the

---

*Three hundreds = 3 × 120 = 360.

most thoughtful and most wise of them. He had heard this news, the killing of his brothers and kinsmen, and it seemed to him he was hit close to home and it seemed to him he could not let such matters sit as the prosecution came most to him. And before assembly was ridden to he calls on the men around Dýrafjorður where his friends and kinsmen were.

A man was called Dýri who was the second greatest aristocrat. He was a great friend of chieftain Þórarinn. His son was called Þorgrímur. He was a full grown man then when this was news.

So it is said of him that he was big and strong, skilled in magic and also the most learned and did much with sorcery.

Þórarinn brought this matter up to his friends and it was their advice all together in this that Þórarinn and Dýri ride to assembly with two hundreds of men, while Þorgrímur Dýri's son volunteered to kill Hávarður and all of them together his kinsmen and companions, he says he has heard that Steinþór of Eyrr had held them in the winter and promised to hold their case to full law with them who were prosecutors with those kinsmen.

Þorgrímur said he knows that Steinþór had ridden from home with a large crowd but the kinsmen and companions had come to Otradalur to Atli, the wretch, Steinþór's in-law, "and nothing will prevent us from killing one on the heels of the other."

That decision was taken that Þorgrímur rides from home as the eighteenth man.* Their trip is not told of before they come to the farm of Atli in Otradalur, that was early one morning and they ride into one little valley which could not be seen from the farm. Then Þorgrímur asked them to dismount, said he was so sleepy that he could no way sit up. They now do so, let the horses graze, but Þorgrímur slept and spread a cloak on his head and was restless in his sleep.

---

*The Icelandic is "*átjánda mann*," which means "eighteenth man." This form is commonly used in the sagas to indicate that a group of that number went together. Here, there were seventeen men with Þorgrímur as the eighteenth.

CHAPTER 20

Now it is to take up what they are doing at home in Otradalur. They sleep in the storehouse in the night which was usual for them. In the morning they wake because Atli was so restless in his sleep that none of them could sleep further because he struggled and blew and beat both hands and feet on the bed until Torfi Valbrandur's son leaped up and waked him and said that no one could sleep because of him and his behavior. Atli sat up and stroked his bald head. Hávarður asks whether anything had been conveyed to him.

He said indeed it was so, "It seemed to me I go out of the storehouse and I saw that wolves run from the south towards the field eighteen together, but in front of the wolves ran a she-fox. It was so sly a creature that I have never seen such before. It was very awful and evil-looking. It looked out and wanted to have eyes on everything and all the animals seemed fierce to me. But when they had come to the farmhouse then Torfi waked me and I knew then certainly that it is the spirits of men. Let us get up at once."

Atli did not abandon his habits, springs up and puts on his shirt, so out like an arrow. And they take their weapons and dress and prepare as swiftly as possible. And when they were all prepared Atli came back and was then wearing a strong mail shirt and a drawn sword in hand.

Then Atli said: "It is most likely that this will go as many have guessed, that it would not help my in-law Steinþór well to have you come down here. Now I request this, that you let me decide for the arrangement of us. It is first my decision that we go out under the housewall and not let them spear us inside. I guess also you do not have in mind to flee, whatever happens."

They say it is so.

CHAPTER 21

It is now to take up that Þorgrímur wakes. He had become warm.

He said then: "I have been to the house for a while and it is so bewildering to me that I do not know what is ahead but we will go to the farmhouse though. I intend that we shall burn them inside. It seems to me that is the quickest way to finish." They now take their weapons and go housewards towards the field.

And when Atli and the others see the men then Atli said: "It is my thought that these are the men of Dýrafjörður and Þorgrímur Dýri's son is in front who is the worst man in all Dýrafjörður and the most skilled in magic. They are the best friends of Þórarinn who has the prosecution about his brother. I intend, even though it be unlikely, to go against Þorgrímur and you Hávarður I intend to go against two. You are tried and a great champion. For Hallgrímur your kinsman, I intend the two who are worth most. For Valbrandur's sons, Torfi and Eyjólfur, I intend four, and for Þorbrandur's sons, Oddur and Þórir, I intend four. For Þorbjörn's sons, Grímur and Þórsteinn, I intend three, and then I intend a man each to both of them Þórhallur and my house servant."

And when Atli had arranged as he wanted Þorgrímur and the others come from the south to the house, see now that the arrangement is other than they supposed. Men stand there with weapons and are prepared to receive them.

Then Þorgrímur said: "Who knows if Atli the womanly* would be more cunning than we suppose but we shall go

---

*Atli is described as "*ragi*," which we translate as "womanly" to preserve the meaning of term and to indicate the contrast with "manly." It is used as a term of abuse and indicates cowardliness. *Grágás* specified that anyone who insulted another with this word could be killed immediately or outlawed.

against them all anyway."

Men now attacked as had been planned. It was the first attack that Atli the little leapt at Þorgrímur and chopped at him two handed with the sword and it did not bite. They chopped at each other a while and it did not bite Þorgrímur.

Then Atli said: "You are like a troll Þorgrímur and not a man when iron does not bite you."

Þorgrímur answered: "How dare you say that, because I chopped at you before as I could and the sword did not bite your bad bald head."

Atli sees that as matters stand it will not do, then throws down the sword and leaps on Þorgrímur and drives him down to the ground. Now his weapon is not by him and he knows that the odds against him are great. It so happens that he bows down to Þorgrímur and bites his windpipe apart, then drags him to where his sword was and slices off his head. After that he looks up and sees that Hávarður has felled one of them who he had to deal with. Atli leaps there first and they do not exchange blows with the other for long before he falls. Hallgrímur had killed both of them who he had to deal with and so had Torfi. Eyjólfur had killed one of the two who he had to deal with. Þórir and Oddur had killed three and one was left. Þorsteinn and Grímur had felled two and one was left. Þórhallur had killed the one which he had to deal with. The houseservant had not killed the one which was intended for him. Hávarður asked them to stop.

Then Þorsteinn Þorbjörn's son said: "My father west in Rauðasandur shall not hear that we brothers do not do our allotted work as other men."

He leaps to one of them with a ax raised and drives it into his head so that he at once got his death.

Atli asked why he should not kill all. Hávarður said that would be for nothing. Atli sat down and asked them to lead them in front of him. He hacked the hair off them and made their heads shaven and then smeared them with tar. Then he took his knife out of the sheath and hacked off all their ears and asked them then so marked to go to meet Dýri and

Þórarinn, said then they will well remember that they had met Atli the little. After that they go from there three, but came eighteen together, all valiantly and well prepared.

Hávarður then said a verse:

Verse 15

> The news came west and from the west
> to the champions in Ísafjörður
> -a sword was reddened in blood
> that the warriors were in a battle,
> Valbrandur's sons from beyond
> shrink back from few things.

After that they go on and bury those who were killed, then take rest and leisure such as they needed.

CHAPTER 22

Now it is to take up when people come to assembly. There was a great crowd. There were great aristocrats and of much worth. There was Gestir Oddleifur's son, Steinþór of Eyrr and Dýri and Þórarinn. There all their cases were talked about together. Steinþór was for Hávarður's side. He offered peace for them and for Gestir Oddleifur's son to decide because he said he knew the most about the case. And because they knew before what was at the bottom of it they went for this very gladly.

Then Gestir said: "Because both want that I talk here a little I shall not be late to do it. I must first take up as was discussed last summer about the killing of Ólafur Hávarður's son that I settle at triple man-price. The killings of Sturla and Þjóðrekur and Ljótur who were killed for no reason shall be discarded. But Þorbjörn Þjóðrekur's son shall have fallen uncompensated for his unfairness and for many unheard-of plots which he has had against Hávarður and many others.

So also those brothers Vakur and Skarfur shall have fallen unprotected.* But their killings shall be even for Brandur the strong's and Ánn's the foster father of Hallgrímur, pay one manprice for Ljótur's follower at Mánaberg who Hávarður and the others had killed. So also about the killing of Ljótur I cannot set a price for it. It is clear to everyone the unfairness that Ljótur had done to Þorbjörn and all others there where he has power. It so happened justly that two children should kill such a champion as Ljótur was. Þorbjörn shall also take that whole meadow freely which they both had together before. But for consolation with Þórarinn shall these men go abroad: Hallgrímur Ásbrandur's son, Torfi and Eyjólfur Valbrandur's sons, Þórir and Oddur Þorbrandur's sons, Þorsteinn and Grímur Þorbjörn's sons. Because you Þórarinn are very old they shall not come back before they hear that you are dead. But Hávarður shall move his living place and not stay in this quarter and also Þórhallur his kinsman. I want you to agree truly to the agreement and there be no tricks from either."

After that Steinþór goes and takes agreement for Hávarður and all his companions with the terms which Gestir had declared. Steinþór then pays also a hundred of silver which was due. Þórarinn and Dýri went to all honorably and said they well liked what was done.

And when this case was closed the earless ones came there to the assembly and tell this news to all within hearing which had happened on their journey. This seemed to all great news and it had gone fittingly. It seemed to people that Þorgrímur had drawn himself to enmity with them and the exchange was fair.

Then Gestir said: "It is thought most true to say that you kinsmen are unlike other people for ill will and unmanliness. Or how was it in your way Þórarinn to pretend as though you

---

*Outlawed. This relates to the concept of the sanctity of the individual, which one gives up for oneself by attacking another (Durrenberger 1992). Anyone could kill an outlaw with impunity.

would settle but go with such trickery? Now because I have talked a little before so that your case may reach forbearance then I let it now stand so according to what was spoken and done before but it would be fitting Þórarinn and Dýri that your case would be very spoiled for your scheming. But because of that in the future I shall never help you in a case. But you Steinþór, accept this because from now I shall help you in your cases with anyone which you have. You have done well and manfully."

Steinþór said that Gestir should have the most say: "It seems to me that they have the worst, have lost many of their men and also their manliness."

After that they break the assembly. Gestir and Steinþór separate with great friendship but Þórarinn and Dýri withstood it very badly.

And when Steinþór came home to Eyrr he sends after them in Otradalur. And when they meet they tell each other what has happened. It seemed to them it had gone very well given what they had had. They thanked Steinþór for the help, said also that his in-law Atli had done well for them and how boldly he had gone in battle and said he was the most bold man. Then there arose the best friendship between the in-laws. Atli was from then on thought the best man wherever he went.

CHAPTER 23

After that Hávarður and the others go home to Ísafjörður. Bjargey rejoices much for them and so the fathers of the brothers and they seemed now to become young a second time.

Now Hávarður decides to prepare for a great feast. There was a great and generous house. Nothing was lacking there. Then he invites Steinþór of Eyrr and his in-law Atli, Gestir Oddleifur's son and all his in-laws and kinsmen. There was a large crowd and the finest feast. They all stay together there a week glad and joyful.

Hávarður was a man very rich in all kinds of wealth and at the close of the feast Hávarður gives Steinþór thirty geldings and five oxen, a shield and a sword and a gold ring, the best treasure. He gave Gestir Oddleifur's son two gold rings and nine oxen. He also gave landowner Atli good gifts. He also gave Valbrandur's sons and Þorbrandur's sons and Þorbjörn's sons all the best of gifts, to some good weapons and other things. He gave to his kinsman Hallgrímur the sword Warflame and with it, very good war weapons, he thanked them all for their good help and honorable bearing. He gave all of them good gifts those who he had invited there because he lacked neither gold nor silver.

And after this feast Steinþór rides home to Eyrr and Gestir to Barðaströnd, Atli to Otradalur. All now separate with the great affection. And they who should go abroad go west to Vaðill and abroad in the summer. They get a good wind, and come to Norway. Earl Hákon then ruled Norway. They were there in the winter and in spring got themselves a ship and lay to plundering and become the most famous men. They have that task some seasons. Now they come out here and Þórarinn was then dead. They become excellent men. There are many sagas of them here in the land and in many other places. Now here closes telling of them.

CHAPTER 24

So it is told of Hávarður that he sells his possessions and they moved north to Svarfaðardalur and up in the valley which is called Oxadalur and builds there his living place and lived there some winters and Hávarður called the farm Hávarðsstaðir.

And some winters later Hávarður heard the news that earl Hákon was dead and king Ólafur Tryggvason came to the land and he had become absolute king over Norway and proclaimed another true belief. And when Hávarður hears

The Saga of Hávarður of Ísafjörður

that he gives up the farm and goes abroad and Bjargey and Þórhallur his kinsman with him. They meet with king Ólafur and he received them well. Hávarður and all of them were then baptized and they were there in the winter in good favor with king Ólafur. That same winter Bjargey expired. But Hávarður and his kinsman Þórhallur went out to Iceland in the summer.

Hávarður brought out with him a great amount of churchwood. He sets his living place in the lower part of Þórhallsdalur and lives there not long before he takes sick, then he calls to Þórhallur his kinsman and said: "The matter now stands that I have got sick which will lead me to death. I want you to inherit my wealth. I grant this to you with good will. You have served me well and given me good help. You shall move your living place to the upper part of Þórhallsdalur. You shall have a church built there and I want you to have me buried therein."

And when he has listed what he wants then he dies a little later. Þórhallur responds quickly and moves his living place up in the valley and builds there a stately house and calls it Þórhallsstaðir. He gets a good wife, and many people have come from him, and lives there until old age. And it is so said that then when Christianity came to Iceland that Þórhallur had a church built at his farm of that wood which Hávarður brought out to here. It was the most splendid building and Hávarður was buried in the church and he was thought to have been the greatest of men.

And there we now close this saga at this time with this matter.

REFERENCES CITED

Amorosi, Thomas. 1989. Contributions to the zooarchaeology of Iceland: some preliminary notes. In Durrenberger and Pálsson 1989:203–227.

Andersson, T.M. and William I. Miller. 1989. *Law and Literature in Medieval Iceland*. Stanford: Stanford University Press.

Byock, Jesse L. 1982. *Feud in the Icelandic Saga*. Berkeley: University of California Press.

———. 1984. Saga form, oral prehistory, and the Icelandic social context. *New Literary History* 16:153–173.

———. 1988. *Medieval Iceland: Society, Sagas and Power*. Berkeley and Los Angeles: University of California Press (Hisarlik Press edition, 1993).

Clover, Carol. 1988. The politics of scarcity: Notes on the sex ratio in early Scandinavia. *Scandinavian Studies* 60:147–188.

Clover, Carol and John Lindow, eds. 1985. *Old Norse-Icelandic Literature: A Critical Guide*. Ithaca: Cornell University Press.

Durrenberger, E. Paul. 1982. *Reciprocity in Gautrek's Saga*

———. 1985. Sagas, totems, and history. *Samfélagstiðindi* 5:51–80.

———. 1991. The Icelandic family sagas as totemic artifacts. In *Social approaches to Viking Studies*, ed. Ross Samson, pp. 11–17. Glasgow: Cruithne Press.

———. 1992. *The Dynamics of Medieval Iceland: Political Economy and Literature*. Iowa City: University of Iowa Press.

Durrenberger, E. Paul and Dorothy Durrenberger. 1986. Translating Gunnlaug's saga: An anthropological approach to literary style and cultural structures. *Translation Review* 21–22:11–20.

References Cited

———. 1992. *The Saga of Gunnlaugur Snake's Tongue.* Farleigh: Dickenson University Press.

Durrenberger, E. Paul, Ástráður Eysteinsson and Dorothy Durrenberger. 1988. Economic representation and narrative structure in *Hænsa Þóris saga. Saga-Book* 22:143–164.

Durrenberger, E. Paul and Gísli Pálsson, eds. 1989. *The Anthropology of Iceland.* Iowa City: University of Iowa Press.

Durrenberger, E. Paul and Jonathan Wilcox. 1992. Humor as a guide to social change: *Bandamanna saga* and heroic values. In *From Sagas to Society: Comparative Approaches to Early Iceland*, ed. Gísli Pálsson, pp. 111–124. Enfield Lock: Hisarlik Press.

Fried, Morton. 1967. *The Evolution of Political Society.* New York: Random House.

Gelsinger, Bruce E. 1981. *Icelandic Enterprise: Commerce and Economy in the Middle Ages.* Columbia: University of South Carolina Press.

Halldórsson, Jón Torfason, Sverrir Tómasson, and Örnólfur Thorsson. 1987. *Íslendinga Sögur og Þættir.* Reykjavík: Svart á Hvítu.

Ingimundarson, Jón Haukur. 1992. Spinning goods and tales: market, subsistence and literary productions. In *From Sagas to Society: Comparative Approaches to Early Iceland*, ed. Gísli Pálsson, 217–230. Enfield Lock: Hisarlik Press.

Jochens, Jenny M. 1980. The church and sexuality in medieval Iceland. *Journal of Medieval History* 6:377–392.

———. 1986. The medieval Icelandic heroine: fact or fiction? *Viator* 17:35–64.

———. 1993. Marching to a different drummer: new trends in medieval Icelandic scholarship: a review article. *Comparative Studies in Society and History* 35:197–207.

Jones, Gwyn. 1935. *Four Icelandic Sagas.* Princeton: Princeton University Press.

Karlsson, Gunnar. 1977. Goðar and höfðingjar in medieval Iceland. *Saga-Book* 19:358–370.

Leach, E.R. 1954. *Political Systems of Highland Burma.* Boston: Beacon.

Lévi-Strauss, Claude. 1966. *The Savage Mind.* Chicago. University of Chicago Press.

Lewellyn, Karl N. and E. Adamson Hoebel. 1941. *The Cheyenne Way: Conflict and Case Law in Primitive Jurisprudence.* Norman: University of Oklahoma Press.

Lin Yueh-hua

———. 1961. *The Lolo of Liang Shan.* New Haven: HRAF Press.

McGovern, T.H. 1990. The archaeology of the Norse North Atlantic. *Annual Review of Anthropology* 19:331–351.

McGovern, T.H., G.F. Bigelow, T. Amorosi, and D. Russel. 1988. Northern islands, human error, and environmental degradation: a view of social and ecological change in the medieval North Atlantic. *Human Ecology* 16:225–270.

Miller, William I. 1990. *Bloodtaking and Peacemaking.* Chicago: University of Chicago Press.

Morris, William and Eiríkur Magnússon. 1891. *The Story of Howard the Halt, The Story of The Banded Men, The Story of Hen Thorir.* The Saga Library Volume 1. London: Bernard Quaritch.

Phillpotts, Bertha S. 1913. *Kindred and Clan in the Middle Ages and After.* Cambridge: Cambridge University Press.

Sahlins, Marshall. 1972. *Stone Age Economics.* New York: Aldine.

Scott, James C. 1991. *Domination and the Arts of Resistance.* New Haven: Yale University Press.

Vígfusson, G. & W. Powell. 1905. *Origines Islandicæ.* Oxford: The Clarendon Press.